D1570324

The Seeker

Translated from the German by

RUTH AND MATTHEW MEAD

MICHAEL HAMBURGER

NELLY SACHS

THE SEEKER
and Other Poems

FARRAR, STRAUS AND GIROUX • New York

Copyright © 1970 by Farrar, Straus and Giroux, Inc.
All rights reserved

Library of Congress catalog card number: 79–137750
SBN 374.2.5780.9
Printed in the United States of America
Published simultaneously in Canada by
Doubleday Canada Ltd., Toronto

First printing, 1970

Designed by Herb Johnson

Selected from Fahrt ins Staublose © Suhrkamp Verlag,
Frankfurt am Main, 1961; Späte Gedichte © Suhrkamp Verlag,
Frankfurt am Main, 1965; and Die Suchende © Suhrkamp Verlag,
Frankfurt am Main, 1966.

"How long," "Chorus of the Wanderers," "Chorus of the
Dead," "Chorus of Invisible Things," "Chorus of Trees,"
and "And the pearly point of eternity" first appeared in
The New Yorker. Grateful acknowledgment is also made to
Antioch Review, The Jewish Spectator, Jewish Life, Mid-
stream, Jewish Heritage, Jewish Exponent, and other
magazines in whose pages a number of these poems have
been published.

Contents

Die Suchende / The Seeker   3

In the Habitations of Death

91250

Eclipse of the Stars

vi

And No One Knows How to Go on

Flight and Metamorphosis

Journey into a Dustless Realm

Death Still Celebrates Life

Glowing Enigmas: IV

xi

The Seeker

Translated by Ruth and Matthew Mead

Die Suchende

1

Von der gewitternden Tanzkapelle
wo die Noten aus ihren schwarzen Nestern fliegen
sich umbringen—
geht die Leidbesessene
auf dem magischen Dreieck des Suchens
wo Feuer auseinandergepflückt wird
und Wasser zum ertrinken gereicht—
Liebende sterben einander zu
durchädern die Luft—

In der Sonnenfinsternis
das Grün ist zu Asche verdammt
die Vögel ersticken in Angst
denn das Ungewisse ist im Annahen—
hinterrücks aus Nacht geschnitten
schleift der Lichttod
des Suchens Geschichte in den Sand—

Seefahrend zum Zenith
wo die weisse Lachmöve sitzt und wartet
kältet sie schon ihren zerfallenden Staub

Sternbild des Geliebten
vom Henker ausgeblasen
der Löwe vom Himmel gefallen—

Sie sucht sie sucht
brennt die Luft mit Schmerz an
die Wände der Wüste wissen von Liebe
die jung in den Abend steigt
diese Vorfeier auf den Tod—

2

The Seeker

1

From the thundering dance-band
where the notes fly from their black nests
suiciding—
the woman possessed by sorrow
walks the magic triangle of seeking
where fire is plucked apart
and water is given for drowning—
lovers die towards each other
veining the air—

In the eclipse of the sun
the green is condemned to ashes
the birds suffocate in fear
for the unknown is approaching—
stealthily the death-by-light
carved out of night
drags into the sand the history of seeking—

Voyaging to the zenith
where the white laughing-gull sits and waits
she already cools her disintegrating dust

Constellation of the beloved
extinguished by the hangman
the lion fallen from the sky—

She searches she searches
ignites the air with pain
the walls of the desert know of love
which climbs new into the evening
the pre-celebration of death—

Sie sucht den Geliebten
findet ihn nicht
muss die Welt neu herstellen
ruft den Engel
eine Rippe aus ihrem Körper zu schneiden
bläst sie mit göttlichem Atem an
weisses Palmenblatt im Schlaf
und die Adern träumend gezogen
Die Suchende in ihrer Armut
nimmt zum Abschied die Krume Erde in den Mund
aufersteht weiter—

2

Du bist der Weissager der Sterne
ihre Geheimnisse fahren aus deiner Unsichtbarkeit
siebenfarbiges Licht aus verschleierter Sonne
Schon ist Tag und Nacht verloren
Neues naht mit Fahnen der Wahrheit
Vulkanische Beichten unter meinen Füssen—

3

Ausgestreut bist du
Same der nirgends häuslich wird
wie kann man Windrichtungen absuchen
oder Farben und Blut
und Nacht die religiöse Angst
Ahnung—der Faden im Labyrinth führt dich—

4

She seeks her beloved
does not find him
must re-create the world
calls on the angel
to cut a rib from her body
blows on it with divine breath
white palm leaf in sleep
and the veins drawn dreaming
The seeker in her poverty
takes the crumb of earth in her mouth as farewell
her resurrection continues—

2

You are the prophet of the stars
their secrets travel out of your invisibility
seven-colored light out of a veiled sun
Day and night is already lost
Something new approaches with flags of truth
Volcanic confessions beneath my feet—

3

You are scattered
seed which settles nowhere
how can one search the ways of the wind
or colors and blood
and night the religious fear
premonition—the thread in the labyrinth leads you—

4

Es ist eine Ungeduld—Waldbrand knistert in den Adern
ruft: wo bist du—mit dem Echo vielleicht im Himmel
und Andere sitzen still an einem Tisch
trinken Milch
draussen der Flieder ist im traurigen Abblühn
der kleine Bruder reitet auf der Ziege—
nur ihr Schmerz sagt ihr dass er tot ist
aber vielleicht hat die Sage ihn unter das Sternbild
des südlichen Kreuzes gestellt
dort wo die Eisprinzessin aus ihrem gefrorenen Grab steigt
ihr Schmuck klappert
er wärmt sie
das Eis fällt ab die strahlenden Jahrtausende
keine Zeit da sie einzusammeln
die Zeit geht in Flammen auf im Scheiterhaufen
brennt ab wenn die Vögel die Nacht aufritzen—

5

Sie sprachen einmal durch die Ferne zueinander
zwei Gefangene
der Henker trug die Stimmen aufgezogen
den Sehnsuchtsweg des Wahnsinns hin und her
Hatte Tod je schönere Geschenke auszutragen—

6

4

It is an impatience—forest fire crackles in the veins
calls: where are you—with the echo perhaps in heaven
and others sit quiet at a table
drinking milk
outside the lilac in its sad fading
the little brother rides upon the goat—
only her pain tells her he is dead
but perhaps the legend has placed him
amid the constellation of the Southern Cross
there where the ice-princess rises from her frozen grave
her jewelry rattles
he warms her
the ice falls off the gleaming millenniums
no time to gather them
time at the stake goes up in flames
burns down when the birds rip open night—

5

Once they spoke to each other through the distance
two prisoners
the hangman bore the voices strung up
back and forth on the road of madness' longing
Had death ever more lovely gifts to deliver—

6

Wo sie steht
ist das Ende der Welt
das Unbekannte zieht ein wo eine Wunde ist
aber Träume und Visionen
Wahnsinn und Schrift der Blitze
diese Flüchtlinge von anderswo her
warten bis Sterben ist geboren
dann reden sie—

7

Was für eine Himmelsrichtung hast du eingenommen
gen Norden ist der Grabstein grün
wächst da die Zukunft
dein Leib ist eine Bitte im Weltall: komm
die Quelle sucht ihr feuchtes Vaterland

gebogen ohne Richtung ist das Opfer—

6

Where she stands
is the end of the world
the unknown enters where a wound is
but dreams and visions
madness and the script of lightnings
these fugitives from somewhere else
wait until dying is born
then they speak—

7

What quarter of the sky have you taken up
to the north the gravestone is green
does the future grow there
your body is a plea in outer space: come
the source seeks its humid fatherland

bent without direction is the victim—

In the Habitations of Death

Translated by Ruth and Matthew Mead

Einer war, der blies den Schofar

Und das Sinken geschieht
um des Steigens willen
                    BUCH SOHAR

Einer war,
Der blies den Schofar—
Warf nach hinten das Haupt,
Wie die Rehe tun, wie die Hirsche
Bevor sie trinken an der Quelle.
Bläst:
Tekia
Ausfährt der Tod im Seufzer—
Schewarim.
Das Samenkorn fällt—
Terua
Die Luft erzählt von einem Licht!
Die Erde kreist und die Gestirne kreisen
Im Schofar,
Den Einer bläst—
Und um den Schofar brennt der Tempel—
Und Einer bläst—
Und um den Schofar stürzt der Tempel—
Und Einer bläst—
Und um den Schofar ruht die Asche—
Und Einer bläst—

Someone blew the Shofar

The sinking occurs for the sake of the rising
BOOK OF SOHAR

Someone
Blew the Shofar—
Threw back his head
As the deer do, as the stags
Before they drink at the spring.
Blows
Tekiah
Death departs in the sigh—
Shewarim
The seed descends—
Terua
The air tells of a light!
The earth circles and the constellations circle
In the Shofar
Which someone blows—
And round the Shofar the temple burns—
And someone blows—
And round the Shofar the temple falls—
And someone blows—
And round the Shofar the ashes rest—
And someone blows—

Hände

Hände
Der Todesgärtner,
Die ihr aus der Wiegenkamille Tod,
Die auf den harten Triften gedeiht
Oder am Abhang,
Das Treibhausungeheuer eures Gewerbes gezüchtet habt.
Hände,
Des Leibes Tabernakel aufbrechend,
Der Geheimnisse Zeichen wie Tigerzähne packend—
Hände,
Was tatet ihr,
Als ihr die Hände von kleinen Kindern waret?
Hieltet ihr eine Mundharmonika, die Mähne
Eines Schaukelpferdes, fasstet der Mutter Rock im Dunkel,
Zeigtet auf ein Wort im Kinderlesebuch—
War es Gott vielleicht, oder Mensch?

Ihr würgenden Hände,
War eure Mutter tot,
Eure Frau, euer Kind?
Dass ihr nur noch den Tod in den Händen hieltet,
In den würgenden Händen?

Hands

Hands
of the gardeners of death,
you who have grown the greenhouse monster of your trade
from the cradle camomile death
which thrives on the hard pastures
or on the slope.
Hands
breaking open the tabernacle of the body,
gripping the signs of the mysteries like tiger's teeth—
Hands,
what did you do
when you were tiny children's hands?
Did you hold a mouth organ, the mane
of a rocking horse, clutch your mother's skirt in the dark,
did you point to a word in a reading book—
Was it God perhaps, or Man?

You strangling hands,
was your mother dead,
your wife, your child?
So that all that you held in your hands was death,
in your strangling hands?

Lange haben wir das Lauschen verlernt!

Ehe es wächst, lasse ich euch es erlauschen
JESAIA

Lange haben wir das Lauschen verlernt!
Hatte Er uns gepflanzt einst zu lauschen
Wie Dünengras gepflanzt, am ewigen Meer,
Wollten wir wachsen auf feisten Triften,
Wie Salat im Hausgarten stehn.

Wenn wir auch Geschäfte haben,
Die weit fort führen
Von Seinem Licht,
Wenn wir auch das Wasser aus Röhren trinken,
Und es erst sterbend naht
Unserem ewig dürstenden Mund—
Wenn wir auch auf einer Strasse schreiten,
Darunter die Erde zum Schweigen gebracht wurde
Von einem Pflaster,
Verkaufen dürfen wir nicht unser Ohr,
O, nicht unser Ohr dürfen wir verkaufen.
Auch auf dem Markte,
Im Errechnen des Staubes,
Tat manch einer schnell einen Sprung
Auf der Sehnsucht Seil,
Weil er etwas hörte,
Aus dem Staube heraus tat er den Sprung
Und sättigte sein Ohr.
Presst, o presst an der Zerstörung Tag
An die Erde das lauschende Ohr,
Und ihr werdet hören, durch den Schlaf hindurch
Werdet ihr hören
Wie im Tode
Das Leben beginnt.

How long have we forgotten how to listen!

Before they spring forth I tell you of them
ISAIAH 42:9

How long have we forgotten how to listen!
He planted us once to listen
Planted us like lyme grass by the eternal sea,
We wanted to grow on fat pastures,
To stand like lettuce in the kitchen-garden.

Although we have business
That leads us far
From his light,
Although we drink tap water,
And only as it dies it reaches
Our eternally thirsting mouths—
Although we walk down a street
Beneath which earth has been silenced
By a pavement,
We must not sell our ears,
Oh, we must not sell our ears.
Even in the market,
In the computation of dust,
Many had made a quick leap
Onto the tightrope of longing,
Because they heard something,
And leapt out of the dust
And sated their ears.
Press, oh press on the day of destruction
The listening ear to the earth,
And you will hear, through your sleep
You will hear
How in death
Life begins.

Lange schon fielen die Schatten.
Nicht sind gemeint jetzt
Jene lautlosen Schläge der Zeit
Die den Tod füllen—
Des Lebensbaumes abgefallene Blätter—

Die Schatten des Schrecklichen fielen
Durch das Glas der Träume,
Von Daniels Deuterlicht erhellt.

Schwarzer Wald wuchs erstickend um Israel,
Gottes Mitternachtssängerin.
Sie verging im Dunkeln,
Namenlos geworden.

O ihr Nachtigallen in allen Wäldern der Erde!
Gefiederte Erben des toten Volkes,
Wegweiser der gebrochenen Herzen,
Die ihr euch füllt am Tage mit Tränen,
Schluchzet es aus, schluchzet es aus
Der Kehle schreckliches Schweigen vor dem Tod.

The shadows fell long ago

The shadows fell long ago.
Here are not meant
Those silent strokes of time
That fill death—
Fallen leaves of the tree of life—

The shadows of terror fell
Through the glass of dreams,
Lit by the prophetic light of Daniel.

Black forest grew suffocatingly round Israel,
God's midnight singer.
She perished in darkness,
Her name lost.

O you nightingales in all the woods of earth!
Plumed heirs of a dead people,
Signpost of broken hearts,
You who fill yourselves by day with tears,
Sob out, sob out
The throat's terrible silence before death.

Die Kerze, die ich für dich entzündet habe

Die Kerze, die ich für dich entzündet habe,
Spricht mit der Luft der Flammensprache Beben,
Und Wasser tropft vom Auge; aus dem Grabe
Dein Staub vernehmlich ruft zum ewgen Leben.

O hoher Treffpunkt in der Armut Zimmer.
Wenn ich nur wüsste, was die Elemente meinen;
Sie deuten dich, denn alles deutet immer
Auf dich; ich kann nichts tun als weinen.

Talking to air in words of flame

Talking to air in words of flame that leap and wave
The candle I have lit for you burns tall,
Water drips from my eye; out of the grave
Your dust calls clearly to the life eternal.

O high encounter in the room of need.
If I but knew what the elements intend;
They define you, for everything indeed
Always defines you; my tears never end.

Nacht, mein Augentrost

Nacht, mein Augentrost du, ich habe meinen Geliebten
    verloren!
Sonne, du trägst sein Blut in deinem Morgen-und Abend-
    gesicht.
O mein Gott, wird wo auf Erden ein Kind jetzt geboren,
Lass es nicht zu, dass sein Herz vor der blutenden Sonne
    zerbricht.

Mörder, aus welchem Grabstaub warst du einmal so schreck-
    lich bekleidet?
Trug ihn ein Wind von einem Stern, den ein Nachtmahr
    behext
Wie Totenschnee hinab auf eine Schar, die sich zu Gott
    hindurchleidet,
Mörder, an deinen Händen zehnfacher Marterpfahl wächst.

Darum auch spürtest du nicht der Liebe Zittern im Morden,
Da sie ein letztes Mal aus soviel Küssen dich angehaucht—
Darum ist ihr, der Hiobzerschlagenen, keine Antwort ge-
    worden,
Die dich zu Ihm wieder, zu Ihm wieder, hätte untergetaucht!

Night, my euphrasy

Night, my euphrasy, I have lost my beloved!
Sun, you bear his blood in your face at dawn and when
    day is done.
Wherever on earth a child is being born now, O God,
Do not allow its heart to break at the sight of the bleeding sun.

Murderer, in what sepulchral dust were you once so grimly
    clad?
Was it borne from a star bewitched by a nightmare, falling
    like the snow
That falls from the dead upon the throng which suffers its
    way to God,
Murderer upon whose hands ten stakes of torture grow.

So that you did not feel the quiver of love as you murdered,
When the final kiss of so many kisses they breathed at you in
    pain—
So that she who was smitten like Job received no answering
    word,
Which would have immersed you again in Him, in Him
    again!

Vielleicht aber braucht Gott die Sehnsucht

Vielleicht aber braucht Gott die Sehnsucht, wo sollte sonst
    sie auch bleiben,
Sie, die mit Küssen and Tränen und Seufzern füllt die
    geheimnisvollen Räume der Luft—
Vielleicht ist sie das unsichtbare Erdreich, daraus die glühen-
    den Wurzeln der Sterne treiben—
Und die Strahlenstimme über die Felder der Trennung, die
    zum Wiedersehn ruft?
O mein Geliebter, vielleicht hat unsere Liebe in den Himmel
    der Sehnsucht schon Welten geboren—
Wie unser Atemzug, ein—und aus, baut eine Wiege für
    Leben und Tod?
Sandkörner wir beide, dunkel vor Abschied, und in das
    goldene Geheimnis der Geburten verloren,
Und vielleicht schon von kommenden Sternen, Monden und
    Sonnen umloht.

But perhaps God needs the longing

But perhaps God needs the longing, wherever else should it
    dwell,
Which with kisses and tears and sighs fills mysterious spaces
    of air—
And perhaps is invisible soil from which roots of stars grow
    and swell—
And the radiant voice across fields of parting which calls to
    reunion there?
O my beloved, perhaps in the sky of longing worlds have been
    born of our love—
Just as our breathing, in and out, builds a cradle for life and
    death?
We are grains of sand, dark with farewell, lost in births'
    secret treasure trove
Around us already perhaps future moons, suns and stars blaze
    in a fiery wreath.

Auch dir, du mein Geliebter

Auch dir, du mein Geliebter,
Haben zwei Hände, zum Darreichen geboren,
Die Schuhe abgerissen,
Bevor sie dich töteten.
Zwei Hände, die sich darreichen müssen
Wenn sie zu Staub zerfallen.
Deine Schuhe waren aus einer Kalbshaut.
Wohl waren sie gegerbt, gefärbt,
Der Pfriem hatte sie durchstochen—
Aber wer weiss, wo noch ein letzter lebendiger
Hauch wohnt?
Während der kurzen Trennung
Zwischen deinem Blut und der Erde
Haben sie Sand hineingespart wie eine Stundenuhr
Die jeden Augenblick Tod füllt.
Deine Füsse!
Die Gedanken eilten ihnen voraus.
Die so schnell bei Gott waren,
So wurden deine Füsse müde,
Wurden wund um dein Herz einzuholen.
Aber die Kalbshaut,
Darüber einmal die warme leckende Zunge
Des Muttertieres gestrichen war,
Ehe sie abgezogen wurde—
Wurde noch einmal abgezogen
Von deinen Füssen,
Abgezogen—
O du mein Geliebter!

Two hands, born to give

Two hands, born to give,
Tore off your shoes
My beloved,
Before they killed you.
Two hands, which will have to give themselves up
When they turn to dust.
Your shoes were made of calfskin.
They were well tanned and dyed,
The awl had pierced them—
But who knows where a last living breath
Still dwells?
During the short parting
Between your blood and earth
They trickled sand like an hourglass
Which fills each moment with death.
Your feet!
The thoughts sped before them.
They came so quickly to God
That your feet grew weary,
Grew sore in trying to catch up with your heart.
But the calfskin
That the warm licking tongue
Of the mother-cow once stroked
Before the skin was stripped—
Was stripped once more
From your feet,
Torn off—
O my beloved!

Du gedenkst der Fusspur

Alles Vergessnen gedenkst du von Ewigkeit her

Du gedenkst der Fusspur, die sich mit Tod füllte
Bei dem Annahen des Häschers.
Du gedenkst der bebenden Lippen des Kindes
Als sie den Abschied von seiner Mutter erlernen mussten.
Du gedenkst der Mutterhände, die ein Grab aushöhlten
Für das an ihrer Brust Verhungerte.
Du gedenkst der geistesverlorenen Worte,
Die eine Braut in die Luft hineinredete zu ihrem toten
    Bräutigam.

You remember the footprint

All that is forgotten you remember from eternity

You remember the footprint which filled with death
As the myrmidon approached.
You remember the child's trembling lips
As they had to learn their farewell to their mother.
You remember the mother's hands which scooped out a grave
For the child which had starved at her breast.
You remember the mindless words
That a bride spoke into the air to her dead bridegroom.

Ich sah eine Stelle

Ich sah eine Stelle, wo ein Herd stand—
Auch fand ich einen Männerhut—
O, mein Geliebter, welcher Sand
Weiss um dein Blut?

Die Schwelle, die liegt ohne Tür
Sie liegt zum Beschreiten bereit—
Dein Haus, mein Geliebter, ich spür
Ist ganz von Gott verschneit.

I found a hat

I found a hat a man had worn—
Saw where a stove had stood—
What sand, O my beloved,
Knows of your blood?

The threshold lies without a door,
Lies waiting to be trod—
The house of him whom I adore
Is all snowed in by God.

Im Morgengrauen

Im Morgengrauen,
Wenn ein Vogel das Erwachen übt—
Beginnt die Sehnsuchtsstunde allen Staubes
Den der Tod verliess.

O Stunde der Geburten,
Kreissend in Qualen, darin sich die erste Rippe
Eines neuen Menschen bildet.

Geliebter, die Sehnsucht deines Staubes
Zieht brausend durch mein Herz.

In the gray dawn

In the gray dawn
When a bird practices awakening—
Begins the hour of longing for all dust
That death deserted.

O hour of births,
Laboring in torments, in which the first rib
Of a new man forms.

Beloved, the longing of your dust
Moves roaring through my heart.

Deine Augen, o du mein Geliebter

Ich sah, dass er sah
JEHUDA ZWI

Deine Augen, o du mein Geliebter,
Waren die Augen der Hindin,
Mit der Pupillen langen Regenbögen
Wie nach fortgezogenen Gottgewittern—
Bienenhaft hatten die Jahrtausende
Den Honig der Gottesnächte darin gesammelt,
Der Sinaifeuer letzte Funken—
O ihr durchsichtigen Türen
Zu den inneren Reichen,
Über denen soviel Wüstensand liegt,
Soviel Qualenmeilen zu o Ihm gehn—
O ihr erloschenen Augen,
Deren Seherkraft nun hinausgefallen ist
In die goldenen Überraschungen des Herrn,
Von denen wir nur die Träume wissen.

34

Your eyes, O my beloved

I saw that he saw
JEHUDA ZWI

Your eyes, O my beloved,
Were the eyes of a hind,
With pupils of long rainbows
As when storms of God are gone—
Bee-like the centuries had stored there
The honey of God's nights,
Last sparks of Sinai's fires—
O you transparent doors
To the inner realms,
Over which so much desert sand lies,
So many miles of torment to reach O Him—
O you lifeless eyes
Whose power of prophecy has fallen
Into the golden astonishments of the Lord,
Of which we know only the dreams.

Die Markthändlerin (B. M.)

Sanfte Tiere zu verkaufen war dein Tun auf einem Markt
    auf Erden,
Lockendes sprachst du wie eine Hirtin zu den Käuferherden.

Umstrahlt von heimkehrenden Fischen im Tränenglorienge-
    wand
Versteckten Füssen der Tauben die geschrieben für Engel
    im Sand.

Deine Finger, das blutge Geheimnis berührend und ab-
    schiedsrot,
Nahmen die kleinen Tode hinein in den riesigen Tod.

The Market Woman (B. M.)

In a market on earth you sold gentle animals,
Spoke temptingly like a shepherdess to buyers who flocked
    round the stalls.

In a gown of tearful glory haloed by fish leaving land
and hidden feet of doves which wrote for angels in sand.

Your fingers, touching the bleeding mystery and red with
    parting breath,
Carried the little deaths into enormous death.

Die Schwachsinnige (B. H.)

Du stiegst auf einen Berg aus Sand
Hilfloses Wandern zu Ihm!
Und glittest hinab; dein Zeichen verschwand.
Für dich stritten die Cherubim.

The Imbecile (B. H.)

You climbed a hill, a sandy one,
A helpless wandering to Him!
Then you slid down; your sign was gone.
For you fought the cherubim.

Der Ruhelose (K. F.)

Alle Landstrassen wurden enger und enger.
Wer war dein Bedränger?

Du kamst nie zum Ziel!
Wie im Ziehharmonikaspiel

Wurden sie wieder auseinandergerissen—
Denn auch im Auge ist kein Wissen.

In die blaue Ferne gehn
Berge und Sterne und Apfelbaumalleen.

Windmühlen schlagen wie Stundenuhren
Die Zeit; bis sie verlöscht die Spuren.

The Restless Man (K. F.)

Narrower and narrower grew each avenue.
Who was it harassed you?

You went on and on!
Like a full-stretched accordion

The closing roads were torn apart again—
The eye does not know how to attain

The blue distance it sees.
Hills and stars, roads with apple trees.

Like clocks striking the hour windmills strike
Until time erases all the tracks alike.

Die Abenteurerin (*A. N.*)

Wohl spieltest du mit nichts als Wasserbällen
Die lautlos an der Luft zerschellen.

Aber das siebenfarbige Licht
Gab jeder sein Gesicht.

Einen Herzschlag nur
Wie Engelflur.

Doch dein letztes Abenteuer—
Still; eine Seele ging aus dem Feuer.

The Adventuress (A. N.)

Although you played with bubbles only
Which burst against air silently.

Yet the seven-colored light which shone
Gave each a face of its own.

Like fields where angels meet
The given heartbeat.

But your last adventure—
Hush; a soul went from the fire.

Die Ertrunkene (*A. N.*)

Immer suchtest du die Perle, am Tage deiner Geburt ver-
loren.
Das Besessne suchtest du, Musik der Nacht in den Ohren.

Meerumspülte Seele, Taucherin du, bis zum Grunde.
Fische, die Engel der Tiefe, leuchten im Licht deiner Wunde.

The Drowned Girl (A. N.)

You always sought the pearl that was lost on the day you saw
      the light.
You sought what is obsessed, in your ears the music of night.

Soul washed by the sea, you diver, touching the sea-deep
      ground.
Fish, angels of the depth, gleam in the light of your wound.

Die alles Vergessende (A. R.)

Aber im Alter ist alles ein grosses Verschwimmen.
Die kleinen Dinge fliegen fort wie die Immen.

Alle Worte vergasst du und auch den Gegenstand;
Und reichtest deinem Feind über Rosen und Nesseln die
    Hand.

The Woman Who Forgot Everything (A. R.)

But in old age all drifts in blurred immensities.
The little things fly off and up like bees.

You forgot all the words and forgot the object too;
And reached your enemy a hand where roses and nettles grew.

Chor der Wandernden

Wir Wandernde,
Unsere Wege ziehen wir als Gepäck hinter uns her—
Mit einem Fetzen des Landes darin wir Rast hielten
Sind wir bekleidet—
Aus dem Kochtopf der Sprache, die wir unter Tränen erlern-
    ten,
Ernähren wir uns.

Wir Wandernde,
An jeder Wegkreuzung erwartet uns eine Tür
Dahinter das Reh, der waisenäugige Israel der Tiere
In seine rauschenden Wälder verschwindet
Und die Lerche über den goldenen Äckern jauchzt.
Ein Meer von Einsamkeit steht mit uns still
Wo wir anklopfen.
O ihr Hüter mit flammenden Schwertern ausgerüstet,
Die Staubkörner unter unseren Wanderfüssen
Beginnen schon das Blut in unseren Enkeln zu treiben—
O wir Wandernde vor den Türen der Erde,
Vom Grüssen in die Ferne
Haben unsere Hüte schon Sterne angesteckt.
Wie Zollstöcke liegen unsere Leiber auf der Erde
Und messen den Horizont aus—

O wir Wandernde,
Kriechende Würmer für kommende Schuhe,
Unser Tod wird wie eine Schwelle liegen
Vor euren verschlossenen Türen!

48

Chorus of the Wanderers

We, the wanderers,
We drag the ways we have come like burdens behind us—
We are clad in the rags of the land
In which we rested—
We feed ourselves from the cooking pot of the language
That we learned with tears.

We, the wanderers,
At every crossroad a door awaits us
Behind which the roe, the orphan-eyed Israel of animals
Vanishes into its murmuring forests
And the lark exults above the golden fields.
A sea of loneliness stands silently beside us
Where we knock.
O you guardians armed with flaming swords,
The grains of dust beneath our wandering feet
Have begun to stir our grandsons' blood—
O we wanderers before the doors of earth,
From saluting into the distance
Our hats have lit up stars.
Like measuring rods our bodies lie on the earth
And measure out the horizon—

O we, the wanderers,
Crawling worms for coming shoes,
Our death will lie like a threshold
Before your tight-shut doors!

Chor der Toten

Wir von der schwarzen Sonne der Angst
Wie Siebe Zerstochenen—
Abgeronnene sind wir vom Schweiss der Todesminute.
Abgewelkt an unserem Leibe sind die uns angetanen Tode
Wie Feldblumen abgewelkt an einem Hügel Sand.
O ihr, die ihr noch den Staub grüsst als einen Freund
Die ihr, redender Sand zum Sande sprecht:
Ich liebe dich.

Wir sagen euch:
Zerrissen sind die Mäntel der Staubgeheimnisse
Die Lüfte, die man in uns erstickte,
Die Feuer, darin man uns brannte,
Die Erde, darin man unseren Abhub warf.
Das Wasser, das mit unserem Angstschweiss dahinperlte
Ist mit uns aufgebrochen und beginnt zu glänzen.
Wir Toten Israels sagen euch:
Wir reichen schon einen Stern weiter
In unseren verborgenen Gott hinein.

Chorus of the Dead

We from the black sun of fear
Holed like sieves—
We dripped from the sweat of death's minute.
Withered on our bodies are the deaths done unto us
Like flowers of the field withered on a hill of sand.
O you who still greet the dust as friend
You who talking sand say to the sand:
I love you.

We say to you:
Torn are the cloaks of the mysteries of dust
The air in which we were suffocated,
The fires in which we were burned,
The earth into which our remains were cast.
The water which was beaded with our sweat of fear
Has broken forth with us and begins to gleam.
We dead of Israel say to you:
We are moving past one more star
Into our hidden God.

Chor der unsichtbaren Dinge

Klagemauer Nacht!
Eingegraben in dir sind die Psalmen des Schweigens.
Die Fusspuren, die sich füllten mit Tod
Wie reifende Äpfel
Haben bei dir nach Hause gefunden.
Die Tränen, die dein schwarzes Moos feuchten
Werden schon eingesammelt.

Denn der Engel mit den Körben
Für die unsichtbaren Dinge ist gekommen.
O die Blicke der auseinandergerissenen Liebenden
Die Himmelschaffenden, die Weltengebärenden
Wie werden sie sanft für die Ewigkeit gepflückt
Und gedeckt mit dem Schlaf des gemordeten Kindes,
In dessen warmem Dunkel
Die Sehnsüchte neuer Herrlichkeiten keimen.

Im Geheimnis eines Seufzers
Kann das ungesungene Lied des Friedens keimen.

Klagemauer Nacht,
Von dem Blitze eines Gebetes kannst du zertrümmert werden
Und alle, die Gott verschlafen haben
Wachen hinter deinen stürzenden Mauern
Zu ihm auf.

Chorus of Invisible Things

Wailing-wall night!
Engraved on you are the psalms of silence.
The footprints, which filled with death
Like ripening apples,
Have found their way home to you.
The tears which moisten your black moss
Are being collected.

Because the angel with the baskets
For invisible things has come.
O the glances of the lovers torn apart
The heaven-creating, the world-bearing
How softly they are plucked for eternity
And covered with the sleep of the murdered child,
In whose warm dark
The longings of new glories germinate.

In the secret of a sigh
The unsung song of peace can germinate.

Wailing-wall night,
You can be smashed by the lightning of a prayer
And all who overslept God
Will wake to him
Behind your falling wall.

Chor der Wolken

Wir sind voller Seufzer, voller Blicke
Wir sind voller Lachen
Und zuweilen tragen wir eure Gesichter.
Wir sind euch nicht fern.
Wer weiss, wieviel von eurem Blute aufstieg
Und uns färbte?
Wer weiss, wieviel Tränen ihr durch unser Weinen
Vergossen habt? Wieviel Sehnsucht uns formte?
Sterbespieler sind wir
Gewöhnen euch sanft an den Tod.
Ihr Ungeübten, die in den Nächten nichts lernen.
Viele Engel sind euch gegeben
Aber ihr seht sie nicht.

Chorus of Clouds

We are full of sighs, full of glances,
We are full of laughter
And sometimes we wear your faces.
We are not far from you.
Who knows how much of your blood rose
And stained us?
Who knows how many tears you have shed
Because of our weeping? How much longing formed us?
We play at dying,
Accustom you gently to death.
You, the inexperienced, who learn nothing in the nights.
Many angels are given you
But you do not see them.

Chor der Bäume

O ihr Gejagten alle auf der Welt!
Unsere Sprache ist gemischt aus Quellen und Sternen
Wie die eure.
Eure Buchstaben sind aus unserem Fleisch.
Wir sind die steigend Wandernden
Wir erkennen euch—
O ihr Gejagten auf der Welt!
Heute hing die Hindin Mensch an unseren Zweigen
Gestern färbte das Reh die Weide mit Rosen um unseren
        Stamm.
Eurer Fusspuren letzte Angst löscht aus in unserem Frieden
Wir sind der grosse Schattenzeiger
Den Vogelsang umspielt—
O ihr Gejagten alle auf der Welt!
Wir zeigen in ein Geheimnis
Das mit der Nacht beginnt.

Chorus of Trees

O all you hunted of the world!
Our speech is mixed from springs and stars
Like yours.
Your letters are of our flesh.
We are the climbing wanderers
We recognize you—
O you hunted of the world!
Today the man like a hind hung on our branches
Yesterday the deer stained the meadows around our trunks
        with roses
The last fear of your footprints is extinguished in our peace,
We are the great shadow-pointer
Played round by birdsong—
O all you hunted of the world!
We point into a secret
Which begins with night.

Chor der Tröster

Gärtner sind wir, blumenlos gewordene
Kein Heilkraut lässt sich pflanzen
Von Gestern nach Morgen.
Der Salbei hat abgeblüht in den Wiegen—
Rosmarin seinen Duft im Angesicht der neuen Toten ver-
    loren—
Selbst der Wermut war bitter nur für gestern.
Die Blüten des Trostes sind zu kurz entsprossen
Reichen nicht für die Qual einer Kinderträne.

Neuer Same wird vielleicht
Im Herzen eines nächtlichen Sängers gezogen.
Wer von uns darf trösten?
In der Tiefe des Hohlwegs
Zwischen Gestern und Morgen
Steht der Cherub
Mahlt mit seinen Flügeln die Blitze der Trauer
Seine Hände aber halten die Felsen auseinander
Von Gestern und Morgen
Wie die Ränder einer Wunde
Die offenbleiben soll ·
Die noch nicht heilen darf.

Nicht einschlafen lassen die Blitze der Trauer
Das Feld des Vergessens.

Wer von uns darf trösten?

Gärtner sind wir, blumenlos gewordene
Und stehn auf einem Stern, der strahlt
Und weinen.

Chorus of Comforters

We are gardeners who have no flowers.
No herb may be transplanted
From yesterday to tomorrow.
The sage has faded in the cradles—
Rosemary lost its scent facing the new dead—
Even wormwood was only bitter yesterday.
The blossoms of comfort are too small
Not enough for the torment of a child's tear.

New seed may perhaps be gathered
In the heart of a nocturnal singer.
Which of us may comfort?
In the depth of the defile
Between yesterday and tomorrow
The cherub stands
Grinding the lightnings of sorrow with his wings
But his hands hold apart the rocks
Of yesterday and tomorrow
Like the edges of a wound
Which must remain open
That may not yet heal.

The lightnings of sorrow do not allow
The field of forgetting to fall asleep.

Which of us may comfort?

We are gardeners who have no flowers
And stand upon a shining star
And weep.

Eclipse of the Stars

Translated by Ruth and Matthew Mead

Engel der Bittenden

Engel der Bittenden,
nun, wo das Feuer wie ein reissendes Abendrot
alles Bewohnte verbrannte zu Nacht—
Mauern und Geräte, den Herd und die Wiege,
die alle abgefallenes Stückgut der Sehnsucht sind—
Sehnsucht, die fliegt im blauen Segel der Luft!

Engel der Bittenden,
auf des Todes weissem Boden, der nichts mehr trägt,
wächst der in Verzweiflung gepflanzte Wald.
Wald aus Armen mit der Hände Gezweig,
eingekrallt in die Feste der Nacht, in den Sternenmantel.
Oder den Tod pflügend, ihn, der das Leben bewahrt.

Engel der Bittenden,
im Wald, der nicht rauscht,
wo die Schatten Totenmaler sind
und die durchsichtigen Tränen der Liebenden
das Samenkorn.
Wie vom Sturm ergriffen, reissen
die mondverhafteten Mütter ihre Wurzeln aus
und mit Knistern der Greise Dürrholz verfällt.
Aber immer noch spielen die Kinder im Sande,
formen übend ein Neues aus der Nacht heraus
denn warm sind sie noch von der Verwandlung.

Engel der Bittenden,
segne den Sand,
lass ihn die Sprache der Sehnsucht verstehn,
daraus ein Neues wachsen will aus Kinderhand,
immer ein Neues!

Angel of supplicants

Angel of supplicants,
now, when the fire like a raging sunset
has burned down into night everything inhabited—
walls and implements, the stove and the cradle,
which are all jettisoned part-loads of longing—
longing, which flies in the blue sail of the air!

Angel of supplicants,
on the white floor of death, which supports nothing now,
grows the forest planted in despair.
Forest of arms with hands for branches,
clawed into the fortress of night, into the cloak of stars.
Or plowing death, death which preserves life.

Angel of supplicants,
in the forest, that does not roar,
where shadows are painters of death
and transparent tears of lovers
the seed.
As if gripped by storm,
the moon-habituated mothers tear out their roots
and dry wood crumbles with an old man's crackle.
But the children are still playing in the sand,
forming, as they practice, something new out of night
for they are still warm from the metamorphosis.

Angel of supplicants,
bless the sand,
let it understand the language of longing,
from which something new wants to grow out of the hands of
        children,
always something new!

O du weinendes Herz der Welt!

O du weinendes Herz der Welt!
Zwiespältig Samenkorn
aus Leben und Tod.
Von dir wollte Gott gefunden werden
Keimblatt der Liebe.

Bist du verborgen in einer Waise,
die am Geländer des Lebens
schwer sich stützend weitergeht?
Wohnst du bei ihr, dort
wo der Stern sein sicherstes Versteck hat?

O du weinendes Herz der Welt!
Auch du wirst auffahren
wenn die Zeit erfüllt ist.
Denn nicht häuslich darf die Sehnsucht bleiben
die brückenbauende
von Stern zu Stern!

O you weeping heart of the world!

O you weeping heart of the world!
Twofold seed
made of life and death.
God wanted to be found by you
seed-leaf of love.

Are you hidden in an orphan girl
who walks on, leaning heavily
on the railing of life?
Do you dwell with her, there
where the star has its safest hiding place?

O you weeping heart of the world!
You too will ascend
when time is fulfilled.
For the longing
that builds bridges
from star to star
must not remain domestic!

Erde

Erde,
alle Saiten deines Todes haben sie angezogen,
zu Ende haben sie deinen Sand geküsst;
der ist schwarz geworden
von soviel Abschied und soviel Tod bereiten.

Oder fühlen sie, dass du sterben musst?
Die Sonne ihr Lieblingskind verlieren wird
und deine Ozeane,
deine schäumenden, lichtentzündeten Wasserpferde
an den Mond geseilt werden,
der in azurgefärbter Nacht
ein neues Becken für die Sehnsucht weiss?

Erde,
viele Wunden schlagen sie in deine Rinde
deine Sternenschrift zu lesen
die in Nächte gehüllt ist bis zu Seinem Thron hinauf.

Aber wie Pilze wachsen die kleinen Tode
an ihren Händen,
damit löschen sie deine Leuchten,
schliessen die Wächteraugen der Cherubim
und die Engel, die Tränenverspäteten, die Goldgräber
in den Schmerzgebirgen,
die Blumen aus dem Blätterwerk Mensch,
haben sie wieder tief unter den Grabsteinen
der Tiergötter vergraben.

Earth

Earth,
they have tightened all the strings of your death,
they have kissed to the last your sand
which has grown black
with preparing so much parting and so much death.

Or do they feel that you must die?
That the sun will lose its favorite child
and that your oceans,
your foaming, light-fired steeds of sea
will be harnessed to the moon
which in azure-colored night
will know a new vessel for longing?

Earth,
they strike many wounds into your crust
to read your starry script
which is cloaked in nights up to His very throne.

But the little deaths grow like fungus
on their hands
with which they quench your lights,
and close the guardian eyes of the cherubim
and they have again buried the angels, the late lamenters,
the diggers for gold in the mountains of pain,
the flowers of the foliage of man,
deep under the gravestones
of the animal gods.

Erde,
wenn auch ihre Liebe ausgewandert ist,
ihre Brände ausgebrannt,
und es leise geworden ist auf dir und leer—

vielleicht augenlose Stelle am Himmel,
darin andere Gestirne zu leuchten beginnen
bienenhaft vom Dufte des Gewesenen angezogen—

so wird dein namenloser Staub, den sie benannt,
dem sie soviele Wandernamen gaben
durch sie ins Gold der Ewigkeit gemünzt
doch seine selige Heimat haben.

Earth,
even if their love has gone into exile,
though their conflagrations are burnt out,
and it has grown quiet upon you and empty—

perhaps an eyeless place in the sky
in which other constellations begin to shine
drawn like bees by the scent of what has been—

so your nameless dust, which they named,
to which they gave so many nomad names
will be minted by them into the gold of eternity
but still have its blessed home.

O ihr Tiere!

O ihr Tiere!

Euer Schicksal dreht sich wie der Sekundenzeiger
mit kleinen Schritten
in der Menschheit unerlösten Stunde.

Und nur der Hahnenschrei,
mondaufgezogen,
weiss vielleicht
eure uralte Zeit!

Wie mit Steinen zugedeckt ist uns
eure reissende Sehnsucht
und wissen nicht was brüllt
im abschiedrauchenden Stall,
wenn das Kalb von der Mutter
gerissen wird.

Was schweigt im Element des Leidens
der Fisch zappelnd zwischen Wasser und Land?

Wieviel kriechender und geflügelter Staub
an unseren Schuhsohlen,
die stehn wie offene Gräber am Abend?

O der kriegszerrissene Leib des Pferdes
an dem fraglos die Fliegen stechen
und die Ackerblume durch die leere Augenhöhle wächst!

O you animals!

O you animals!

Your fate turns like the second-hand
with small steps
in the unredeemed hour of mankind.

And only the cockcrow,
wound up by the moon,
knows perhaps
your ancient time!

As if covered with stones
is your violent longing to us
and we do not know what bellows
in the smoking stable of parting
when the calf is torn
from its mother.

How does the fish, struggling between water and land,
keep silent in the element of suffering?

How much creeping and winged dust
on the soles of our shoes,
which stand like open graves at evening?

Oh, the horse's war-torn body
where flies without question sting
and the wildflower grows through the empty eye socket!

Nicht der sterndeutende Bileam
wusste von eurem Geheimnis,
als seine Eselin
den Engel im Auge behielt!

Not even Balaam, prophet of the star,
knew of your secret
as his ass
beheld the angel!

Golem Tod!

Golem Tod!
Ein Gerüst ist gestellt
und die Zimmerleute gekommen
und wie die Meute der Hunde
lechzend,
laufen sie deiner Schattenspirale nach.

Golem Tod!
Nabel der Welt,
dein Skelett breitet die Arme
mit falschem Segen!
Deine Rippen legen sich auf die Breitengrade der Erde
richtig zugemessen!

Golem Tod!
Am Bette des Waisenkindes
stehen die vier Cherubim
mit vorgeschlagenen Flügeln,
angesichtsverhüllt—
während auf den Feldern
das Kraut der Entzweiung gepflanzt wird
und verfallene Gärtner
am Mond die Äpfel reifen lassen!

Am Sternenhimmel aber wiegt
der Greis mit der Waage
das weinende Ende
von der Wolke zum Wurm!

74

Golem death!

Golem death!
A scaffold is prepared
and the carpenters are come
and like a pack of hounds
slavering,
they track your shadow-spiral.

Golem death!
Navel of the world,
your skeleton spreads its arms
in false blessing!
You lay your ribs along earth's latitudes
fitting exactly!

Golem death!
Four cherubim stand
by the bed of the orphan child
wings folded forward
hiding their faces—
while in the fields
the weed of dissension is planted
and worn-out gardeners
let apples ripen on the moon!

But in the starry sky
the old man with the scales
weighs the weeping end
from the cloud to the worm!

Golem Tod!
Niemand aber vermag dich zu heben
aus der Zeit hinaus—
denn geborgt ist dein Rauschblut
und dein eisenumschütteter Leib
zerfällt mit allem Kehricht
wieder in den Beginn!

In den Ruinen aber wohnt doppelte Sehnsucht!
Der Stein umschläft grün mit Moos sich
und Sternblumen im Gras
und goldene Sonnen auf Stengeln entstehn.

Und in den Wüsten
sieht man Schönes in der Ferne,
und wer die Braut verlor
umarmt die Luft,
denn nicht kann Geschaffenes ganz zugrunde gehn—

Und alle entgleisten Sterne
finden mit ihrem tiefsten Fall
immer zurück in das ewige Haus.

Golem death!
But no one can lift you
out of time—
for the blood of your frenzy is borrowed
and your ironbound body
crumbles with all debris
back into the beginning!

But in the ruins dwells double longing!
The stone sleeps itself green with moss
and starwort in the grass
and golden suns on stems arise.

And in the deserts
beauty is seen in the distance,
and whoever lost the bride
embraces air,
for what was created cannot entirely perish—

And every star that fails
finds with its deepest fall
the way back to the eternal home.

Geschirmt sind die Liebenden

Geschirmt sind die Liebenden
unter dem zugemauerten Himmel.
Ein geheimes Element schafft ihnen Atem
und sie tragen die Steine in die Segnung
und alles was wächst
hat nur noch eine Heimat bei ihnen.

Geschirmt sind die Liebenden
und nur für sie schlagen noch die Nachtigallen
und sind nicht ausgestorben in der Taubheit
und des Waldes leise Legenden, die Rehe,
leiden in Sanftmut für sie.

Geschirmt sind die Liebenden
sie finden den versteckten Schmerz der Abendsonne
auf einem Weidenzweig blutend—
und üben in den Nächten lächelnd das Sterben,
den leisen Tod
mit allen Quellen, die in Sehnsucht rinnen.

The lovers are protected

The lovers are protected
beneath the walled-up sky.
A secret element gives them breath
and they bear the stones into the blessing
and all that grows
has a homeland only with them.

The lovers are protected
and only for them the nightingales sing
and have not died out in deafness
and the deer, soft legends of the forest,
suffer in meekness for them.

The lovers are protected
they find the hidden pain in the evening sun
bleeding on a willow branch—
and smilingly in the nights they practice dying
the quiet death
with all springs which run in longing.

Abraham

O du
aus dem mondversiegelten Ur,
der du im Sande der abtropfenden Sintfluthügel
die sausende Muschel
des Gottesgeheimnisses fandst—

O du
der du aus dem weinenden Sternbild Babylons
den Äon des lebenden Lebens hobst—
das Samenkorn des himmlischen Landmannes warfst
bis in den feurigen Abend des Heute darin die Ähre brennt.

O du
der aus Widderhörnern die neuen Jahrtausende geblasen
bis die Weltenecken sich bogen im Heimwehlaut—

O du
der die Sehnsucht an den Horizont der unsichtbaren Himmel
heftete
die Engel in die Länder der Nacht berief—
die Beete der Träume bereitete
für die Schar der sich übersteigenden Propheten—

O du
aus dessen ahnendem Blut
sich das Schmetterlingswort *Seele* entpuppte,
der auffliegende Wegweiser ins Ungesicherte hin—

Abraham

O you
out of moon-sealed Ur,
you who found the roaring seashell
of God's mystery
in the sand of the dune draining after the flood—

O you
who lifted the aeon of living life
from Babylon's weeping constellation—
cast the seed of the heavenly yeoman
even into this present fiery evening where the ear of corn is
      burning.

O you
who blew the new millennia from the rams' horns
until the corners of the world curved in a sound of longing
      for home—

O you
who nailed longing on the horizon
of invisible skies
called the angels into the lands of night—
who prepared the flowerbeds of dreams
for the troop of prophets outdoing each other—

O you
out of whose presaging blood
burst the butterfly word *soul,*
the signpost taking wing into incertitude—

O du
aus Chaldäas Sterndeuterhafen
unruhige Welle, die in unseren Adern
noch immer sucht voll Tränen ihr Meer.

O Abraham,
die Uhren aller Zeiten,
die sonnen- und monddurchleuchteten
hast du auf Ewigkeit gestellt—

O dein wunderbrennender Äon,
den wir mit unseren Leibern ans Ende bringen müssen—
dort, wo alle Reife hinfällt!

O you
restless wave from Chaldea's
port of starry prophecy, which full of tears
still seeks its sea in our veins.

O Abraham
you have set at eternity
the clocks of all the ages,
lit by sun and moon—

O your aeon burning with wonders
which we with our bodies must consummate—
there, where all ripeness falls!

Jakob

O Israel,
Erstling im Morgengrauenkampf
wo alle Geburt mit Blut
auf der Dämmerung geschrieben steht.
O das spitze Messer des Hahnenschreis
der Menschheit ins Herz gestochen,
o die Wunde zwischen Nacht und Tag
die unser Wohnort ist!

Vorkämpfer,
im kreissenden Fleisch der Gestirne
in der Nachtwachentrauer
daraus ein Vogellied weint.

O Israel,
du einmal zur Seligkeit endlich Entbundener—
des Morgentaus tröpfelnde Gnade
auf deinem Haupt—

Seliger für uns,
die in Vergessenheit Verkauften,
ächzend im Treibeis
von Tod und Auferstehung

und vom schweren Engel über uns
zu Gott verrenkt
wie du!

Jacob

O Israel,
Firstborn in the grapple of gray morning
where all birth is written with blood
upon the dawn.
O the pointed knife of cockcrow
thrust in the heart of mankind,
O the wound between night and day
which is our dwelling place!

Champion,
in the travailing flesh of constellations
in the sorrow of the nightwatch
from which a birdsong weeps.

O Israel
you born at last to bliss—
the dripping grace of the morning dew
upon your head—

More blissful for us,
sold in forgetfulness,
groaning in the drifting ice
of death and resurrection

and disabled to God
by the heavy angel above us
like you!

Daniel

Daniel, Daniel—
die Orte ihres Sterbens
sind in meinem Schlaf erwacht—
dort, wo ihre Qual mit dem Welken der Haut verging
haben die Steine die Wunde
ihrer abgebrochenen Zeit gewiesen—
haben sich die Bäume ausgerissen
die mit ihren Wurzeln
die Verwandlung des Staubes
zwischen Heute und Morgen fassen.

Sind die Verliese mit ihren erstickten Schreien
aufgebrochen,
die mit ihrer stummen Gewalt
den neuen Stern gebären helfen—
ist der Weg mit den Hieroglyphen ihrer Fusspuren
in meine Ohren gerieselt
wie in Stundenuhren,
die der Tod erst wendet.

O die gräberlosen Seufzer in der Luft,
die sich in unseren Atem schleichen—
Daniel, Daniel,
wo bist du schreckliches Traumlicht?
Der ungedeuteten Zeichen sind zu viele geworden—

O wir Quellenlose,
die wir keine Mündung mehr verstehn,
wenn sich das Samenkorn im Tode
des Lebens erinnert—

Daniel

Daniel, Daniel—
the places where they died
have awakened in my sleep—
there, where their torment passed from them as their skin
        wrinkled,
stones have shown the wounds
of their discontinued time—
the trees have torn themselves up
which with their roots
clutch the metamorphosis of dust
between today and tomorrow.

Are the dungeons broken open
by their suffocated cries,
which help to give birth to the new star
with their dumb force—
has the way with the hieroglyphics of their footprints
trickled into my ears
as in hourglasses
which are only turned by death.

O the graveless sighs in the air
which creep into our breath—
Daniel, Daniel,
where are you terrible dreamlight?
The uninterpreted signs have become too many—

O we without a source,
we who understand a mouth no more,
when the seed in death
remembers life—

Daniel, Daniel,
vielleicht stehst du zwischen Leben und Tod
in der Küche, wo in deinem Schein
auf dem Tische liegt
der Fisch mit den ausgerissenen Purpurkiemen,
ein König des Schmerzes?

Daniel, Daniel,
perhaps you stand between life and death
in the kitchen, where in your light
the fish with the torn-out purple gills
lies on the table,
a king of pain?

Aber deine Brunnen

Aber deine Brunnen
sind deine Tagebücher
o Israel!

Wieviel Münder hast du geöffnet
im vertrockneten Sand,
die Scheibe des Todes abgeschnitten
vom lebenden Leben.

Wieviel leuchtende Wurzeln der Sehnsucht
hast du aus der Tiefe gehoben
wieviel Gestirnen hast du Spiegel aufgetan,
ihr Geschmeide in den dunkel
weinenden Schlaf gelegt.

Denn deine Brunnen
sind deine Tagebücher
o Israel!

Als Abraham grub in Ber Seba
heftete er mit sieben Schwüren
den Namen seines Herrn
in die Heimat des Wassers.

Ihr, durch das Fleisch der Erde Dürstenden,
viele Begegnungen sind euch aufbewahrt
im fliessenden Gebetschrein der Brunnen.
Gesicht des Engels
über Hagars Schulter geneigt

But your wells

But your wells
are your book of days
O Israel!

How many mouths have you opened
in the parched sand,
the slice of death cut off
from living life.

How many glowing roots of longing
have you lifted from the depth
for how many constellations have you opened mirrors,
laying their jewelry into the dark
weeping sleep.

For your wells
are your book of days
O Israel!

When Abraham dug in Beersheba
he nailed the name of his god
with seven oaths
into the home of water.

You who thirst through the flesh of earth,
many encounters are preserved for you
in the wells' flowing shrine of prayer.
The angel's face
bending over Hagar's shoulder

wie eine Nebelhaut
ihren Tod fortblasend.

Redender Fels mit der bitteren
Wasserzunge zu Mara,
die mit verlorenem Geheimnis getaucht
zur Süsse sich wandelte—

Deine Tagebücher
sind in die leuchtenden Augen
der Wüsten geschrieben
o Israel!

Schlagrutenhaft
dein Herz zuckt
wo die Schalen der Nacht
eine Brunnentiefe halten,
darunter die Landschaften Gottes
zu blühen beginnen,
die du, Erinnernder unter den Völkern,
hinaufhebst
mit dem Krug deines Herzens—
hinaufhebst
in die brunnenlosen Räume
der Vergessenheit!

blowing her death away
like a skin of mist.

Rock speaking to Mara
with the bitter tongue of water
which dipped with a lost secret
changed to sweetness—

Your book of days
is written into the shining eyes
of the deserts
O Israel!

As if struck by a rod
your heart quivers
where the bowls of night
hold the depths of a well
beneath which the landscapes of God
begin to bloom,
which you, rememberer among the nations,
lift up
with the vessel of your heart—
lift up
into the spaces of forgetfulness
where no wells are!

Sinai

Du Truhe des Sternschlafs
aufgebrochen in der Nacht,
wo alle deine Schätze,
die versteinten Augen der Liebenden,
ihre Münder, Ohren, ihr verwestes Glück
in die Herrlichkeit gerieten.
Rauchend vor Erinnerung schlugst du aus
da die Hand der Ewigkeit deine Sanduhr wendete—
die Libelle im Bluteisenstein
ihre Schöpferstunde wusste—

Sinai
von deinem Gipfel
Moses trug,
schrittweise abkühlend
den geöffneten Himmel
an seiner Stirn herab,
bis die im Schatten Harrenden
das unter dem schützenden Tuche Brodelnde
schauernd ertrugen—

Wo ist noch ein Abkömmling
aus der Erschauerten Nachfolge?
O so leuchte er auf
im Haufen der Erinnerungslosen,
Versteinten!

Sinai

You ark of starry sleep
broken open in the night,
where all your treasures,
the petrified eyes of the lovers,
their mouths, ears, their putrefied happiness
moved into glory.
Smoking with memory you struck out
as the hand of eternity turned your hourglass—
as the dragonfly in the blood-ironstone
knew the hour of its creator—

Sinai
down from your peak
Moses bore the opened sky
on his forehead
cooling step by step
until they who waited in the shadow
were able to bear, trembling,
what shone beneath the veil—

Is there still an heir
to the succession of them that trembled?
Oh, may he glow
in the crowd of them that do not remember,
of the petrified!

David

Samuel sah
hinter der Blindenbinde des Horizontes—
Samuel sah—
im Entscheidungsbereich
wo die Gestirne entbrennen, versinken,
David den Hirten
durcheilt von Sphärenmusik.
Wie Bienen näherten sich ihm die Sterne
Honig ahnend—

Als die Männer ihn suchten
tanzte er, umraucht
von der Lämmer Schlummerwolle,
bis er stand
und sein Schatten auf einen Widder fiel—

Da hatte die Königszeit begonnen—
Aber im Mannesjahr
mass er, ein Vater der Dichter,
in Verzweiflung
die Entfernung zu Gott aus,
und baute der Psalmen Nachtherbergen
für die Wegwunden.

Sterbend hatte er mehr Verworfenes
dem Würmertod zu geben
als die Schar seiner Väter—
Denn von Gestalt zu Gestalt
weint sich der Engel im Menschen
tiefer in das Licht!

David

Samuel saw
behind the blindfold of the horizon—
Samuel saw—
in the realm of decision,
where the constellations ignite, sink,
David the shepherd
quickened by music of the spheres.
The stars came to him like bees
sensing honey—

As the men sought him
he danced, surrounded by smoke
from the lambs' sleepy wool,
till he stood
and his shadow fell on a ram—

The age of kings had begun—
But in the year he came of age
he measured out in despair,
a father of poets,
the distance to God,
and built inns of night from the psalms
for those left by the way.

Dying he had more depravity
to give to wormy death
than all his forefathers—
For from form to form
the angel in man weeps itself
deeper into the light!

Saul

Saul, der Herrscher, abgeschnitten vom Geiste
wie eine Brennschnur erloschen—

Einen Fächer von Fragen tragend in der Hand—
das Wahrsageweib mit der Antwort, auf Nachtgaloschen

beunruhigt den Sand.
Und Samuels, des Propheten Stimme,

gerissen aus dem Lichterkreis
spricht wie verwelkte Erinnerung in die Luft—

und das Licht wie eine verzückte Imme
sein Ausgefahrnes in die Ewigkeit ruft.

Über Saul, dem Herrscher, steht eine Krone aus Sterben—
und das Weib liegt wie vom Lichte verbrannt—

und die Macht wird ein armer Luftzug erben
und legt sie zu einem Haupteshaar in den Sand.

Saul

Saul, the ruler, cut off from the spirit
extinguished like a burning fuse—

Carrying a fan of questions in the hand—
the witch with the answer, in night shoes

disturbs the sand.
And Samuel's, the voice of prophecy,

torn from the circle of lights
speaks like a withered memory into the air—

and the light like an ecstatic bee
calls into eternity his soul that was elsewhere.

Above Saul, the ruler, hangs a crown of dying—
and the woman lies as if burnt by the light's glare—

And a poor breeze, heir to the power, will lay it sighing
into the sand beside a single hair.

Geheime Grabschrift

O welche Rune schreibt der Erdenschoss
mit einer Eiche qualverbogenem Geäst
in diese Luft, die Zeit mit Schreckenmuster malt.

Greis mit dem Kaftan—
Mantel aus der grossen Einsamkeit geschnitten,
von vielen Tod- und Weihekerzen angeraucht—
Greis in der heimatlosesten der Sprachen seufzend—

Der eiserne Soldat liess dich in Wellen
an dem Baume leiden,
nachschaffend eine windverrenkte Erdenflucht.

Zenit des Schmerzes!
Harfend Tränenholz
und Krähen die den Sterbebissen kauen
den Grausamkeit noch übrig liess—

Vielleicht ist hier die Stelle
wo dieser Stern, die schwarzversiegelte
Geheimnisfülle sprengt
und furchtbar überkocht
in unfassbare Ewigkeit hinein!

Secret Epitaph

Oh, what rune does the womb of earth
inscribe with an oak's torment-twisted branches
upon this air, which paints time with patterns of terror.

Old man with the caftan—
Coat cut from the great loneliness,
smoky with many candles of death and consecration—
Old man sighing in the most homeless of languages—

The iron soldier let you suffer in waves
at the tree,
re-creating a wind-twisted flight from earth.

Zenith of pain!
Wooden harp of tears
and crows chewing the morsel of death
which cruelty left over—

Perhaps this is the place
where this star will burst the black-sealed
abundance of secrets
and boil over monstrously
into inconceivable eternity!

Wir sind so wund

Wir sind so wund,
dass wir zu sterben glauben
wenn die Gasse uns ein böses Wort nachwirft.
Die Gasse weiss es nicht,
aber sie erträgt nicht eine solche Belastung;
nicht gewöhnt ist sie einen Vesuv der Schmerzen
auf ihr ausbrechen zu sehn.
Die Erinnerungen an Urzeiten sind ausgetilgt bei ihr,
seitdem das Licht künstlich wurde
und die Engel nur noch mit Vögeln und Blumen spielen
oder im Traume eines Kindes lächeln.

We are so stricken

We are so stricken
that we think we're dying
when the street casts an evil word at us.
The street does not know it,
but it cannot stand such a weight;
it is not used to seeing a Vesuvius of pain
break out.
Its memories of primeval times are obliterated,
since the light became artificial
and angels only play with birds and flowers
or smile in a child's dream.

Wir Mütter

Wir Mütter,
Sehnsuchtsamen aus Meeresnacht
holen wir heim,
Heimholerinnen sind wir
von verstreutem Gut.

Wir Mütter,
träumerisch
mit den Gestirnen wandelnd,
lassen uns die Fluten
von Gestern und Morgen,
mit unserer Geburt
wie mit einer Insel
allein.

Wir Mütter
die wir zum Tode sagen:
Blühe auf in unserem Blut.
Die wir Sand zum Lieben bringen
und den Sternen eine spiegelnde Welt—

Wir Mütter,
die wir in den Wiegen
die dämmernden Erinnerungen
des Schöpfertages wiegen—
des Atemzuges Auf und Ab
ist unseres Liebessanges Melodie.

Wir Mütter
wiegen in das Herz der Welt
die Friedensmelodie.

We mothers

We mothers,
we gather seed of desire
from oceanic night,
we are gatherers
of scattered goods.

We mothers,
pacing dreamily
with the constellations,
the floods
of past and future,
leave us alone
with our birth
like an island.

We mothers
who say to death:
blossom in our blood.
We who impel sand to love and bring
a mirroring world to the stars—

We mothers,
who rock in the cradles
the shadowy memories
of creation's day—
the to and fro of each breath
is the melody of our love long.

We mothers
rock into the heart of the world
the melody of peace.

Immer

Immer
dort wo Kinder sterben
werden die leisesten Dinge heimatlos.
Der Schmerzensmantel der Abendröte
darin die dunkle Seele der Amsel
die Nacht heranklagt—
kleine Winde über zitternde Gräser hinwehend
die Trümmer des Lichtes verlöschend
und Sterben säend—

Immer
dort wo Kinder sterben
verbrennen die Feuergesichter
der Nacht, einsam in ihrem Geheimnis—
Und wer weiss von den Wegweisern
die der Tod ausschickt:
Geruch des Lebensbaumes,
Hahnenschrei der den Tag verkürzt
Zauberuhr vom Grauen des Herbstes
in die Kinderstuben hinein verwunschen—
Spülen der Wasser an die Ufer des Dunkels
rauschender, ziehender Schlaf der Zeit—

Immer
dort wo Kinder sterben
verhängen sich die Spiegel der Puppenhäuser
mit einem Hauch,
sehen nicht mehr den Tanz der Fingerliliputaner
in Kinderblutatlas gekleidet;
Tanz der stille steht

Always

Always
there where children die
the quietest things become homeless.
The sunset's cloak of pain
in which the blackbird's dark soul
sadly heralds the night—
small winds blowing across trembling grasses
extinguishing the debris of light
and sowing death—

Always
there where children die
the fiery faces of the night
burn out, lonely in their mystery—
And who knows of the signposts
that death sends out:
smell of the tree of life,
cockcrow that shortens the day
magic clock enchanted into nurseries
by the horror of autumn—
water lapping on the shore of darkness
whispering, tugging sleep of time—

Always
there where children die
doll's house mirrors cloud over
with a breath,
see no more the dance of the finger-midgets
clad in child's-blood satin;
dance that stands still

wie eine im Fernglas
mondentrückte Welt.

Immer
dort wo Kinder sterben
werden Stein und Stern
und so viele Träume
heimatlos.

like a world in a telescope
shifted to the moon.

Always
there where children die
stone and star
and so many dreams
become homeless.

Trauernde Mutter

Nach der Wüste des Tages,
in der Oase des Abends,
über die Brücke welche
die Liebe sich über zwei Welten weinte,
kam dein toter Knabe.
Alle deine versunkenen Luftschlösser
die Scherben deiner flammenversehrten Paläste,
Gesänge und Segnungen
untergegangen in deiner Trauer,
umfunkeln ihn wie eine Feste,
die der Tod nicht eingenommen hat.

Sein milchbetauter Mund,
seine Hand, die deine überholt hat,
sein Schatten an der Zimmerwand
ein Flügel der Nacht,
mit der gelöschten Lampe heimwärtssinkend—
am Strande zu Gott
hingestreut wie Vogelbrocken in ein Meer
des Kindesgebetes Echolaut
und übern Rand des Schlafs gefallener Kuss—
O Mutter, Erinnernde,
nichts ist mehr dein
und alles—
denn die stürzenden Sterne suchen
durch die Mohnfelder der Vergessenheit
auf ihrem Heimweg dein Herz,
denn alle deine Empfängnis
ist hilfloses Leid.

Mourning Mother

After the desert of day,
in the oasis of evening,
your dead boy came
across the bridge
which love had wept between two worlds.
All your sunken castles in air
the shards of your flame-seared palaces,
songs and blessings
drowned in your sorrow,
sparkled around him like a fortress
unconquered by death.

His milk-bedewed mouth,
his hand which has outreached yours,
his shadow on the wall of the room
a wing of night,
sinking homewards with the extinguished lamp—
strewn for God
on the shore like crumbs for birds into a sea
the echo of the child's prayer
and the kiss fallen over the rim of sleep—
O mother, rememberer,
nothing more is yours
and everything—
for the falling stars on their way home
search for your heart
in the poppy fields of oblivion,
for all your conceiving
is helpless suffering.

Abschied

Abschied—
aus zwei Wunden blutendes Wort.
Gestern noch Meereswort
mit dem sinkenden Schiff
als Schwert in der Mitte—
Gestern noch von Sternschnuppensterben
durchstochenes Wort—
Mitternachtgeküsste Kehle
der Nachtigallen—

Heute—zwei hängende Fetzen
und Menschenhaar in einer Krallenhand
die riss—

Und wir Nachblutenden—
Verblutende an dir—
halten deine Quelle in unseren Händen.
Wir Heerscharen der Abschiednehmenden
die an deiner Dunkelheit bauen—
bis der Tod sagt: schweige du—
doch hier ist: weiterbluten!

Farewell

Farewell—
word bleeding from two wounds.
Yesterday still a word of the sea
with the sinking ship
as sword in the middle—
Yesterday still a word
pierced by the dying of shooting stars—
midnight-kissed throat
of the nightingales—

Today—two hanging shreds
and human hair in a clawing hand
that tore—

And we who bleed in aftermath—
bleeding to death because of you—
hold your source in our hands.
We hosts who bid farewell
who build your darkness—
until death says: be silent—
but here it is: go on bleeding!

Land Israel

Land Israel,
deine Weite, ausgemessen einst
von deinen, den Horizont übersteigenden Heiligen.
Deine Morgenluft besprochen von den Erstlingen Gottes,
deine Berge, deine Büsche
aufgegangen im Flammenatem
des furchtbar nahegerückten Geheimnisses.

Land Israel,
erwählte Sternenstätte
für den himmlischen Kuss!

Land Israel,
nun wo dein vom Sterben angebranntes Volk
einzieht in deine Täler
und alle Echos den Erzvätersegen rufen
für die Rückkehrer,
ihnen kündend, wo im schattenlosen Licht
Elia mit dem Landmanne ging zusammen am Pfluge,
der Ysop im Garten wuchs
und schon an der Mauer des Paradieses—
wo die schmale Gasse gelaufen zwischen Hier und Dort
da, wo Er gab und nahm als Nachbar
und der Tod keines Erntewagens bedurfte.

Land Israel,
nun wo dein Volk
aus den Weltenecken verweint heimkommt
um die Psalmen Davids neu zu schreiben in deinen Sand

Land of Israel

Land of Israel,
your bounds once measured out
by your saints surmounting the horizon.
Your morning air enchanted by God's firstborn,
your mountains, your bushes
gone up in the breath of flame
of the terribly close-come mystery.

Land of Israel,
chosen starry place
for the celestial kiss!

Land of Israel,
now when your people seared by dying
move into your valleys
and all echoes call the patriarchs' blessing
for those returning,
proclaiming to them where in the shadowless light
Elijah walked with the yeoman at the plow,
where hyssop grew in the garden
and even by the wall of paradise—
where the small alley ran between here and there
there where He gave and took as neighbor
and death needed no cart for harvest.

Land of Israel,
now when your people
come home from the corners of the world with tear-stained
          eyes
to write the psalms of David anew in your sand

und das Feierabendwort *Vollbracht*
am Abend seiner Ernte singt—

steht vielleicht schon eine neue Ruth
in Armut ihre Lese haltend
am Scheidewege ihrer Wanderschaft.

and that afterwork word *finished*
sings on the evening of its harvest—

perhaps a new Ruth is already standing
in poverty holding her gleanings
at the crossroad of her wandering.

Aus dem Wüstensand

Aus dem Wüstensand holst du deine Wohnstatt wieder heim.
Aus den Jahrtausenden, die liegen in Goldsand verwandelt.

Aus dem Wüstensand treibst du deine Bäume wieder hoch
die nehmen die Quellen hin zu den Sternen—

Aus dem Wüstensand in den soviel Schlaf einging
vom Volke Israel

ziehst du der Schafe Schlummerwolle an den Tag.
Mit der Erinnerung als Rutengänger

gräbst du die versteckten Blitze der Gottesgewitter aus,
wälzt die Steine zum Bethaus

Steine, die fester Schlaf um die magische Nacht
von Beth-El sind,

und gefrorene Zeit um der Heimwehleitern Gespross.
Am Abend aber, wenn die Erde ihre letzte Melodie

am Horizont spielt und die Brunnen dunkle Rahelaugen
       sind,
öffnet Abraham den blauen Himmelsschrein

darin die funkelnde Tiara des Tierkreises ruht,
Israels ewige Siegertrophäe

an die schlafenden Völker der Welt.

Out of the desert sand

Out of the desert sand you bring your dwelling place home
     again.
Out of the millennia which lie transformed in sand of gold.

Out of the desert sand you thrust up your trees again
they take the wells up to the stars—

Out of the desert sand into which so much sleep
of Israel's people entered

you draw the sleepy wool of sheep to the light.
With memory as dowser

you dig out the hidden lightnings of God's storms,
roll the stones to the temple

stones, which are deep sleep around the magic night
of Beth-el,

and frozen time around the ladder rungs of homesickness.
But at evening when earth plays its last melody

on the horizon and the wells are dark eyes of Rachel
Abraham opens the blue shrine of the sky

in which the sparkling tiara of the zodiac rests,
Israel's eternal trophy of victory

to the sleeping peoples of the world.

Frauen und Mädchen Israels

Frauen und Mädchen Israels,
das mit dem Schlafstrauch besäte Land
ist aufgebrochen an euren Träumen—

In der Küche backt ihr Kuchen der Sara
denn immer wartet ein anderes draussen!—
Wiegt, was die Gründe vorgewogen haben

mischt, was von Gestirnen gemischt wurde
und was der Landmann ans Ende brachte.
Die Sehnsucht der Erde greift nach euch

mit dem Duft des geöffneten Gewürzschreines.
Die Dudaimbeere im Weizenfelde, die, seit Ruben
sie fand, ins Unsichtbare gewachsen war,

rötet sich wieder an eurer Liebe.

Aber die Wüste, die grosse Wegwende zur Ewigkeit hin,
die mit ihrem Sande schon die Stundenuhr
der Mondzeit zu füllen begonnen hatte,

atmet über den verschütteten Fusspuren
der Gottgänger, und ihre verdorrten Quelladern
füllen sich mit Fruchtbarkeit—

denn euer Schatten, Frauen und Mädchen Israels,
strich über ihr brennendes Goldtopasgesicht
mit dem Frauensegen—

Women and girls of Israel

Women and girls of Israel,
the land sown with the bush of sleep
is broken open by your dreams—

In the kitchen you bake the cake of Sarah
for something else is always outside waiting!—
Weigh what reasons have weighed before

mix what was mixed by constellations
and what the yeoman completed.
The longing of earth reaches for you

with the scent of the opened shrine of spices.
Mandrake in the cornfield, which, since Reuben
found it, had grown into invisibility,

reddens again with your love.

But the desert, the great bend in the road to eternity,
which had already begun to fill with its sand
the hourglass of lunar time,

breathes above the filled-in footsteps
of those who go to God, and its parched veined springs
fill with fertility—

for your shadow, women and girls of Israel,
swept across its golden topaz face
with the women's blessing—

Über den wiegenden Häuptern der Mütter
öffnen sich zur Nachtzeit wieder
der Hirtengestirne Blütenzweige
singen in der Kinder warmen Schlaf
die ewigen Verwandlungen zu Gott hinein.
Die heimatlosen Jahrtausende
die seit dem Brande des Tempels umherirrten
ungeliebt in der Stundenuhr des Staubes
schlagen aus in neuer Herrlichkeit
in den Betten der Kinder
frische Äste überwinterter Bäume.

Above the rocking heads of the mothers

Above the rocking heads of the mothers
the blossom branches of the shepherds' stars
open again at night
singing in the warm sleep of children
the eternal transformations up to God.
The homeless millennia
which since the burning of the temple roamed about
unloved in the hourglass of dust
break forth in new glory
in the children's beds
fresh branches of the trees surviving winter.

Die ihr in den Wüsten

Die ihr in den Wüsten
verhüllte Quelladern sucht—
mit gebeugten Rücken
im Hochzeitslicht der Sonne lauscht—
Kinder einer neuen Einsamkeit mit Ihm—

Eure Fusspuren
treten die Sehnsucht hinaus
in die Meere aus Schlaf—
während euer Leib
des Schattens dunkles Blumenblatt auswirft
und auf neugeweihtem Land
das zeitmessende Zwiegespräch
zwischen Stern und Stern beginnt.

You who seek

You who seek hidden
veins of water in the desert—
listening with bent backs
in the nuptial light of the sun—
children of a new loneliness with Him—

Your footprints
tread longing
into the seas of sleep—
while your bodies
cast the shadow's dark petal
and on newly consecrated land
the time-measuring dialogue
between star and star begins.

O meine Mutter

O meine Mutter,
wir, die auf einem Waisenstern wohnen—
zu Ende seufzen den Seufzer derer
die in den Tod gestossen wurden—
wie oft weicht unter deinen Schritten der Sand
und lässt dich allein—

In meinen Armen liegend
kostest du das Geheimnis
das Elia bereiste—
wo Schweigen redet
Geburt und Sterben geschieht
und die Elemente anders gemischt werden—

Meine Arme halten dich
wie ein hölzerner Wagen die Himmelfahrenden—
weinendes Holz, ausgebrochen
aus seinen vielen Verwandlungen—

O meine Rückkehrerin,
das Geheimnis verwachsen mit Vergessenheit—
höre ich doch ein Neues
in deiner zunehmenden Liebe!

O my mother

O my mother,
we who dwell on an orphan star—
sighing to the end the sighs of those
who were thrust into death—
how often the sand gives way beneath your steps
and leaves you alone—

Lying in my arms
you taste the mystery
Elijah knew—
where silence speaks
birth and death occur
and the elements are mixed differently—

My arms hold you
as a wooden cart holds those ascending to heaven—
weeping wood, broken out
from its many transformations—

O you who return,
the mystery overgrown with forgetting—
I still hear something new
in your increasing love!

Aber in der Nacht

Aber in der Nacht,
wenn die Träume mit einem Luftzug
Wände und Zimmerdecken fortziehn,
beginnt die Wanderung zu den Toten.
Unter dem Sternstaub suchst du sie—

Deine Sehnsucht baut an der Schwester—
aus den Elementen, die sie verborgen halten,
holst du sie herein
bis sie aufatmet in deinem Bett—
der Bruder aber ist um die Ecke gegangen
und der Gatte zu hoch schon eingekehrt
da lässt die Demut dich verstummen—

Aber dann—wer hat die Reise unterbrochen—
beginnt die Rückkehr—
Wie der kleinen Kinder Wehklagen
erschrocken an der Erde
bist du—
der Tod der Toten ist mit der Zimmerdecke
herabgesunken—
schützend liegt mein Kopf auf deinem Herzen
die Liebe—zwischen dir und dem Tod—

So kommt die Dämmerung
mit dem roten Sonnensamen hingestreut
und die Nacht hat sich ausgeweint
in den Tag—

But in the night

But in the night,
when dreams pull away
walls and ceilings with a breath of air,
the trek to the dead begins.
You search for them under the stardust—

Your longing builds up your sister—
from the elements which keep her hidden,
you bring her in
till she sighs with relief in your bed—
but your brother has gone round the corner
and your husband sits in too high a place
so that humility makes you silent—

But then—who has broken the journey—
the return begins—
like little children wailing
you are
frightened on the earth—
the death of the dead has sunk down
with the ceiling—
my head lies on your heart protectingly
love—in between you and death—

Thus dawn comes
strewn with the red seed of the sun
and night has cried itself out
into the day—

Chassidische Schriften

Es heisst: die Gebote der Thora entsprechen der Zahl
der Knochen des Menschen, ihre Verbote der Zahl der Adern.
So deckt das ganze Gesetz den ganzen Menschenleib.

Alles ist Heil im Geheimnis
und das Wort lief aus
das atemverteilende Weltall,

schützt wie Masken mit seiner abgewandten Seite
die sternegebärende Nacht.

Alles ist Heil im Geheimnis
und lebendig aus der Quelle
wuchs die Sehnsucht

durch die Geschöpfe.
Namen bildeten sich
wie Teiche im Sand.

Alles ist Heil im Geheimnis
und die Knochen leben die magische Zahl der Gebote
und die Adern bluten sich zu Ende

wie Sonnenuntergang,
einmal übertretend die Gesetze im Schmerz.

Alles ist Heil im Geheimnis
und lebt aus der Erinnerung
und aus Vergessenheit graut der Tod.

Und die Bundeslade zog ihre Träger
über den Jordan, denn die Elemente trieben
geschwisterhaft die Segnung der Schrift!

Hasidic Scriptures

*It is said: the commandments of the Torah equal the number
of a man's bones, its prohibitions the number of the veins.
Thus the whole law covers the whole human body.*

All is salvation in the mystery
and the word went forth
the breath-dispensing universe

protects like masks with its side turned away
the night giving birth to stars.

All is salvation in the mystery
and lively from the source
longing grew

through the creatures.
Names formed
like pools in the sand.

All is salvation in the mystery
and the bones live the magic number of the commandments
and the veins bleed to the end

like sunset,
transgressing once the laws of pain.

All is salvation in the mystery
and lives from memory
and death threatens from forgetfulness.

And the ark of the covenant drew its bearers
across the Jordan, for the elements drove
like kith and kin the blessing of the scripture!

Und das Herz der Steine,
flugsandangefüllt,
ist der Mitternächte Aufbewahrungsort
und der begrabenen Blitze Wohnstatt

Und Israel, der Horizontenkämpfer
schläft mit dem Sternensamen
und den schweren Träumen zu Gott!

And the heart of stones,
filled with quicksand,
is the place where midnights are stored up
and the dwelling place of buried lightning

And Israel, the fighter of horizons
sleeps with the seed of stars
and the heavy dreams towards God!

Zuweilen wie Flammen

Zuweilen wie Flammen
jagt es durch unseren Leib—
als wäre er verwoben noch mit der Gestirne
Anbeginn.

Wie langsam leuchten wir in Klarheit auf—

O nach wieviel Lichterjahren haben sich unsere
Hände gefaltet zur Bitte—
unsere Kniee sich gesenkt—
und aufgetan sich unsere Seele
zum Dank?

Rushing at times like flames

Rushing at times
like flames through our bodies—
as if they were still woven with the beginning
of the stars.

How slowly we flash up in clarity—

Oh, after how many lightyears have our hands
folded in supplication—
our knees bent—
and our souls opened
in thanks?

Wie Nebelwesen

Wie Nebelwesen
gehen wir durch Träume und Träume
Mauern von siebenfarbigem Licht
durchsinken wir—

Aber endlich farblos, wortlos
des Todes Element
im Kristallbecken der Ewigkeit
abgestreift aller Geheimnisse Nachtflügel . . .

Like beings of mist

Like beings of mist
we walk through dreams and dreams
we sink through walls
of seven-colored light—

But colorless at last, wordless
the element of death
in the crystal vessel of eternity
stripped off the nightwings of all mysteries . . .

Engel auf den Urgefilden

Engel auf den Urgefilden
die ihr den Anfang losbindet,
die Weissagungen in die Elemente sät
bis die Fruchtknoten der Gestirne
sich rűnden
und wieder die Monde des Todes
die abnehmende Tonleiter singen—

Und in staubiger Nachtwache
der Mensch die Arme wild
zum Himmel wirft
und *Gott* sagt
und die Dunkelheit
in einer Veilchenträne duftet—

Engel auf den Urgefilden
wieviel Martermeilen
muss die Sehnsucht, zurück
zu eurem Segensraum durcheilen!

Angels upon the primeval fields

Angels upon the primeval fields
you who unbind the beginning,
sowing the prophecies into the elements
until the pistils of the constellations
round
and again the moons of death
sing down the scale—

And in the dusty nightwatch
man throws his arms wildly
up to heaven
and says *God*
and in the tear of a violet
the darkness smells—

Angels upon the primeval fields
how many tormented miles
must longing hurry back through
to your blessed space!

Wer weiss, welche magischen Handlungen

Wer weiss, welche magischen Handlungen
sich in den unsichtbaren Räumen vollziehn?

Wieviel glühende Rosen der Beschwörung
auf den Gewehrmündungen der Krieger blühn?

Welche Netze die Liebe knüpft
über einem bleichen Krankengesicht?

Manch einer hörte seinen Namen rufen
am Scheideweg

und kämpfte handlos in der Heiligen Scharen.
O die Brunnen, gebohrt in die Luft

daraus Prophetenwort trinkt,
und ein Staubvergrabener plötzlich seinen Durst löscht.

Welche Saaten an den Gestirnen des Blutes erwachsen
welche Missernten des Kummers.

Und der Heiligen Lese aus Licht.
Ringmauern für die schwärzesten Taten.

Friedhöfe für die Martern
der bis auf den Gottgrund zerrissenen Opfer.

O die unsichtbaren Städte
darin die Schlafenden ihre Ausflüge machen—

Wälder der Traumgesichte—
was werdet ihr sein in Wahrheit nach unserem Tod?

Who knows what magic acts

Who knows what magic acts
occur in the invisible rooms?

How many glowing roses of invocation
bloom on the rifle barrels of the soldiers?

What nets love knots
above a pale sick face?

Many have heard their names called
where the road forks

and fought without hands in the company of saints.
O the wells, bored into the air,

from which words of prophets drink
and a man buried in dust suddenly quenches his thirst.

What seeds growing on the constellations of the blood
what failed harvests of grief.

And the saints' vintage of light.
Ramparts for the blackest deeds.

Cemeteries for the torments of
the victims torn to the very depth of God.

O the invisible cities
in which the sleepers make their excursions—

Forests of visions—
what will you be in truth after our death?

Musik in den Ohren der Sterbenden—
Wenn die Wirbeltrommel der Erde
leise nachgewitternd auszieht—
wenn die singende Sehnsucht der fliegenden Sonnen,
die Geheimnisse deutungsloser Planeten
und die Wanderstimme des Mondes nach dem Tod
in die Ohren der Sterbenden fliessen,
Melodienkrüge füllend im abgezehrten Staub.

Staub, der offen steht zur seligen Begegnung,
Staub, der sein Wesen auffahren lässt,
Wesen, das sich einmischt in die Rede
der Engel und Liebenden—
und vielleicht schon eine dunkle Sonne
neu entzünden hilft—
denn alles stirbt sich gleich:
Stern und Apfelbaum
und nach Mitternacht
reden nur Geschwister—

Music in the ears of the dying

Music in the ears of the dying—
When the rolling drum of earth
takes the field soft as a dying storm—
when the singing desire of flying suns,
the secrets of meaningless planets
and the wandering voice of the moon after death
flow into the ears of the dying,
filling vessels of melody in the emaciated dust.

Dust, which stands open to blissful encounter,
Dust, that lets its being ascend,
Being, that mingles in the talk
of angels and lovers—
and is helping perhaps
to ignite anew
a dark sun—
for everything dies in the same way:
star and apple tree
and after midnight
only kith and kin speak—

Im Lande Israel

Nicht Kampfgesänge will ich euch singen
Geschwister, Ausgesetzte vor den Türen der Welt.
Erben der Lichterlöser, die aus dem Sande
aufrissen die vergrabenen Strahlen
der Ewigkeit.
Die in ihren Händen hielten
funkelnde Gestirne als Siegestrophäen.

Nicht Kampflieder
will ich euch singen
Geliebte,
nur das Blut stillen
und die Tränen, die in Totenkammern gefrorenen,
auftauen.

Und die verlorenen Erinnerungen suchen
die durch die Erde weissagend duften
und auf dem Stein schlafen
darin die Beete der Träume wurzeln
und die Heimwehleiter
die den Tod übersteigt.

I do not want to sing you battle hymns,
brothers and sisters, outcasts standing before the doors of the
    world.
Heirs of the redeemers of light, who tore out of the sand
the buried rays
of eternity.
Who held in their hands
sparkling constellations as trophies of victory.

I do not
want to sing you battle songs,
beloved,
only stanch the blood
and thaw out the tears
which froze in the death chambers.

And seek the lost memories
which smell prophetically through the earth
and sleep on the stone
in which root the flowerbeds of dreams
and the ladder of homesickness
which transcends death.

Wenn im Vorsommer

Wenn im Vorsommer der Mond geheime Zeichen aussendet,
die Kelche der Lilien Dufthimmel verströmen,
öffnet sich manches Ohr unter Grillengezirp
dem Kreisen der Erde und der Sprache
der entschränkten Geister zu lauschen.

In den Träumen aber fliegen die Fische in der Luft
und ein Wald wurzelt sich im Zimmerfussboden fest.

Aber mitten in der Verzauberung spricht eine Stimme klar
        und verwundert:
Welt, wie kannst du deine Spiele weiter spielen
und die Zeit betrügen—
Welt, man hat die kleinen Kinder wie Schmetterlinge,
flügelschlagend in die Flamme geworfen—

und deine Erde ist nicht wie ein fauler Apfel
in den schreckaufgejagten Abgrund geworfen worden—

Und Sonne und Mond sind weiter spazierengegangen—
zwei schieläugige Zeugen, die nichts gesehen haben.

When in early summer

When in early summer the moon sends out secret signs,
the chalices of lilies scent of heaven,
some ear opens to listen
beneath the chirp of the cricket
to earth turning and the language of spirits set free.

But in dreams fish fly in the air
and a forest takes firm root in the floor of the room.

But in the midst of enchantment a voice speaks clearly and
        amazed:
World, how can you go on playing your games
and cheating time—
World, the little children were thrown like butterflies,
wings beating into the flames—

and your earth has not been thrown like a rotten apple
into the terror-roused abyss—

And sun and moon have gone on walking—
two cross-eyed witnesses who have seen nothing.

And No One Knows
How to Go on

Translated by Ruth and Matthew Mead

Da du unter dem Fuss dir

Da du
unter dem Fuss dir
das staubbeflügelte Sternbild der Flucht gebarst
warf eine Hand Feuer in deinen Mund.

O eingeschlossenes Liebeswort
du brennende Sonne
im Rad der Nacht—

O meine Sonne
ich töpfre dich herein
in meiner Liebe Sternfallverlies
ins Asyl meiner Atemzüge
dieser leisesten Selbstmörderschar.

Beize mein Licht
mit der Ozeane unbehüteten Salzflucht,
ziehe Windkundschaft ein
aus der knospenden Landschaft der Seele.

Mit Lippen am Stein des Gebets
küsse ich lebenslang Tod,
bis der singende Samen aus Gold
den Fels der Trennung zerbricht.

As you gave birth beneath your foot

As you
gave birth beneath your foot
to the dust-winged constellation of fleeing
a hand thrust fire into your mouth.

O locked-in word of love
you burning sun
in the wheel of night—

O my sun
I imprison you
in my love's dungeon of falling stars
in the sanctuary of my breath
this quietest pack of suicides.

My light! cauterize
with the unguarded salt-flight of the oceans,
draw knowledge of the wind
from the budding landscape of the soul!

With lips at the stone of prayer
I kiss death all life long,
until the singing seed of gold
splits the rock of parting.

Wurzeln schlagen

Wurzeln schlagen
die verlassenen Dinge
in den Augen Fliehender,

und die Tür, die offensteht,
schweigt mit dem verlorenen Stimmband
an des Zimmers leerer Kehle.

Suppentopf ist eine Insel
ohne Flutbegehr der Münder,

Schreibtisch ohne Sternenkunde.
Meteore tief im Nachtgrab

liegen Briefe ungelesen
doch ihr Bergkristallbeschwerer

glüht an einer Fenstersonne—
denn mit Wolken schreibt der Schreiber:

Rose

schon an einen neuen Himmel
und die Antwort fiel in Asche.

Bienenflügel in dem Glassarg
strahlt in Gold die Flucht durch Gräber,

wird mit der zerrissnen Sehnsucht
schmelzen an dem Honigfeuer,

wenn Nacht sich endlich auf den Scheiterhaufen wirft.

Forsaken things

Forsaken things
strike root
in the eyes of the fugitives,

and the door that stands open
is silent with the lost vocal chord
at the room's empty throat.

a soup dish is an island
without the mouths desiring the flood,

desk without astronomy.
Metcor-deep in the grave of night

letters lie unread
but their rock-crystal paperweight

glows by a window-sun—
for the writer is already writing:

Rose

with clouds on a new sky
and the answer fell to ashes.

Bee wing in the glass coffin
irradiates in gold the flight through graves,

will melt with torn longing
at the honey fire,

when night at last casts itself on the pyre.

Gebogen durch Jahrtausende

Traumgebogen weit, weiter
sternenrückwärts in der Erinnerung,
schlafwassergefahren
durch gekrümmte Staubsäulen,
des Landes Kanaan heidnischen Sand küssend,
der anders gesiebt mit durstigen Göttern
doch Wüste mit Honig und Milchgeschmack.

Dieses Bündel Sonnengestrahle,
ein Riese legte es ab von der Schulter
und hinein
in Abrahams Laubhüttenhand.

Die zuckte golddurchstochen.

Und wieder ein Strahlenfinger,
hoch zeigend durch Bibelnacht
auf Tyrannenwort,
Rizpa,
das Muttergestirn,
gehorsam ihrer Herzader,
liess Schakale abfallen
wie Mondwasser
von der Söhne über
den Tod verurteilten Leichenhaut.

Tiefer in Aschenzeit,
auch Antigone
siebte Freiheit
im Echo des Staubes—

Bent through Millennia

Bent far by dreams, farther
backward to stars in the memory,
sailing waters of sleep
through twisted pillars of dust,
kissing the heathen sand of the land of Canaan
which sifted differently with thirsty gods
is still desert with the taste of milk and honey.

This bundle of sunrays,
a giant put it down from his shoulder
and into
Abraham's tabernacle-hand.

Which twitched pierced by gold.

And again a finger of radiance
pointing high through Bible-night
at the word of tyranny,
Rizpah,
the mother-constellation
obedient to her heart's vein,
shook off jackals
like moonwater
from the corpse-skin
of the sons
condemned beyond death.

Deep in ashen time,
Antigone too
sifted freedom
in the echo of dust—

In der Schattenecke
meergrau im Ysop
schnuppert der Esel,
blaugeträumt das Auge
vor Engelsentzücken.

Nachtverbunden lehnt Bileam
neben unbegriffner Sendung.

Klage, Klage, Klage
in Harfen, Weiden, Augen,
und Tempel nur noch im Feuer!

Israel, knisternde Fahne im Salz,
und die Flucht abgeschnitten
mit des Meeres weinendem Schwert
oder
im Angstschweiss vergraben
an einer Mauer, rauchend vor Jägerdurst.

Flucht, Flucht, Flucht,
Fluchtmeridiane verbunden
mit Gott-Sehnsuchts-Strichen—

Flucht aus den schwarzgebluteten Gestirnen
des Abschieds,
Flucht in die blitztapezierten
Herbergen des Wahnsinns,

Flucht, Flucht, Flucht
in den Gnadenstoss der Flucht
aus der zersprengten Blutbahn
kurzer Haltestelle—

In the corner of shadow
the ass, sea gray,
sniffs in the hyssop,
the eye dreamy-blue
with angelic delight.

Linked to night Balaam leans
beside an uncomprehended message.

Lament, lament, lament
in harps, willows, eyes,
and temples only now in the fire!

Israel, creaking flag in the salt,
and the flight cut off
by the weeping sword of the sea
or
buried in cold sweat
at a wall, smoking with hunter's thirst.

Flight, flight, flight,
meridians of flight linked
with lines of God's longing—

Flight from the black-bled constellations
of farewell,
Flight into the lightning-papered
shelters of madness,

Flight, flight, flight
into the *coup de grâce* of flight
from the short halting place
on the blown-up line of blood—

Auswanderer-Schritte

Auswanderer-Schritte
Pulsreise-Schritte
betten sich in Landsflucht
weit hinter dem Meilenstein,
der verwaist im Tage wacht.

O wie sie reisen
auf dem Faden des Schlafes
mit des Atems Adamzügen
hin zu den Spiegeln
geklärte mit Blindenasche
für Balschem-Blicke,
daran Gott nicht zerbricht.
Erinnerungsversengte
salzige Flügel
vor der Pforte,
die mit erstem Lebenslicht
beschrieben ist.

O der Peiniger,
der hier uns in Scherben warf
am abschiedsschwarzen Kinderfelsen
ins gestirnlose Meer.

Immigrant steps

Immigrant steps
Pulsing journey steps
embed themselves far behind
the milestone on the road to exile,
which, orphaned, keeps vigil by day.

Oh, how they journey
on the thread of sleep
with Adam's gasping breath
to the mirrors
cleared for Baalshem stares
with the ashes of the blind,
mirrors at which God does not shatter.
Salt wings
singed by memory
before the portal
which is inscribed
with the first light of life.

O the tormentor
who cast us here in fragments,
at the child's rock, black with farewell,
into the starless sea

Was suchst du Waise

Was suchst du Waise
in der Erde noch
die Eiszeit deiner Toten fühlend—
die blauen Monde
erhellen schon die fremde Nacht.

Schneller als Wind
mischt Tod die schwarzen Karten
vielleicht ein Regenbogen
abgelöst vom Fischgeschupp
nun deines Vaters Augen schloss,
Meersalz und Tränen
in der Vergängnis Totenbinde.

Vielleicht
der Mutter fortgefallner Kuss
im Staubgebrüll
des Löwenrachens ruht?

Der Henker
in der schuldbeladenen Finsternis
hat seinen Finger tief im Haar
des Neugeborenen versteckt
das knospet Lichterjahre schon
in ungeträumte Himmel fort.

Der Erde Nachtigallenzunge
singt
in deine Hände—Waise—
die in des Sandes
schwarzgewordnem Abschied suchen

Orphan, what do you still seek

Orphan, what do you
still seek in earth
feeling the ice age of your dead—
the blue moons
already light the strange night.

Swifter than wind
death shuffles the black cards
perhaps a rainbow
peeled from scales of fish
closed your father's eyes,
sea salt and tears
in the blindfold of mortification.

Perhaps
your mother's lost kiss
rests in the dusty roar
of the lion's jaws?

The hangman
in the guilt-laden darkness
has hidden his finger deep
in the hair of the newborn child
which has budded for lightyears
into undreamed heavens.

The nightingale tongue of earth
sings
into your hands—orphan—
which search the sand's
blackened farewell

Geliebtes suchen

das längst
aus scharfgesägtem
Sterngebiss
entschwand—

searching for what is loved

which vanished
long ago
from the sharply sawn
teeth of stars—

Ein schwarzer Jochanaan

Ein schwarzer Jochanaan,
Nachtfetzen behangen,
schleift an Gestirnmusik
den weissen Sehnsuchtsdorn,

sticht ihn durch der Mondmeere Schlafleib,
zieht die Rückwege
des Heimwehs,
diese schmerzende Nabelschnur
durch der Adern seufzende
Sternstrassen,

immer hinter dem Rücken
des Schneeläufers Tod.

A black Jochanaan

A black Jochanaan,
hung with shreds of night,
sharpens the white thorn of longing
on the music of the stars,

pierces the sleeping body of moon-seas,
drawing the returning roads
of homesickness,
this aching navel-string,
through the sighing orbits
of the veins,

always behind the back
of the snow-runner death.

Eine Windschleppe

Eine Windschleppe
mit den Atemzügen der Toten.
Der Angler zieht den Silberfisch hoch
durch die wirkliche Engelgesellschaft.

Gebet der blutigen Kiemen.

Aber beim Gottesdienst
die alten Frauen schlafen
trotz des Lavendelduftes
und den in Brand geratenen Buchstaben
die ihnen die Augen beizen—

A silken train of wind

A silken train of wind
with the breathing of the dead.
The angler hauls high the silver fish
through the real company of angels.

Prayer of the bloody gills.

But in church
the old women sleep
in spite of the scent of lavender
and letters which have caught fire
and make their eyes water—

Ein Licht über dem See

Alles was auszieht aus Tod
hat sein Leben in unsichtbaren Figuren vollbracht

Ein Licht über dem See.
Zeichen des Pfeils, eingegraben
in der Holzwand der Hütte—
schon schmerzt Auferstehung.

Eine Rotbrust voller Unruhe,
zirpend am Fenster—
an der Silbergrube
Skelett der Erde aufgeworfen—
ein Hund bellt darüber fort—

Aber der Zusammenhang
liegt eingerollt
in der Gebetskapsel eines Frommen,
dem die Scherben gekittet wurden
mit der Gnade Wundbalsam—

A light above the lake

*All that departs out of death
has completed its life in invisible forms*

A light above the lake.
Sign of the arrow carved
into the hut's wooden wall—
resurrection already hurts.

A robin full of unrest
twittering at the window—
at the silvermine
earth's skeleton cast up—
a dog barking above it—

But the correlation
lies rolled up
in the pious man's phylactery
for whom the fragments were glued together
with the balm of grace—

Als der Blitz

Als der Blitz
das Gebäude des Glaubens entzündete
wanderten Füsse über dem Wasser
und Arme strichen wie Fittiche in der Luft.

Nur die Schwermut
der Wein gekeltert
für die Kirchhofsengel
die einmal ausschlafen sollen
floss zurück in die Erde.

When lightning

When lightning
set on fire the edifice of faith
feet walked above the water
and arms beat like pinions in the air.

Only melancholy
the wine trodden
for the churchyard angels
who ought to sleep late for once
flowed back into the earth.

Kain!

Kain! um dich wälzen wir uns im Marterbett:
Warum?
Warum hast du am Ende der Liebe
deinem Bruder die Rose aufgerissen?

Warum den unschuldigen Kindlein
verfrühte Flügel angeheftet?
Schnee der Flügel
darauf deine dunklen Fingerabdrücke
mitgenommen
in die Wirklichkeit der Himmel schweben?

Was ist das für eine schwarze Kunst
Heilige zu machen?
Wo sprach die Stimme
die dich dazu berief?

Welche pochende Ader
hat dich ersehnt?

Dich
der das Grün der Erde
zum Abladeplatz trägt

Dich
der das Amen der Welt
mit einem Handmuskel spricht—

Kain—Bruder—ohne Bruder—

Cain!

Cain! because of you we toss on the bed of torture:
Why?
Why at the end of love
did you tear open your brother's rose?

Why did you fasten premature wings
to the innocent children?
Snow of wings
on which your dark fingerprints
are carried swaying
into the reality of the heavens?

What kind of black magic
makes saints?
Where did the voice
that called you speak?

What pulsing vein
yearned for you?

You
who carry the green of earth
to the rubbish heap

You
who speak the world's Amen
with the muscle of your hand—

Cain—brother—without brother—

Erwachen

Erwachen—
Vogelstimmen
aus dem Brunnen der Nacht
Wasserzählen der Zeit—
Abend-Morgenstern
bleicher Same
dornengespitzt
streut Tod in Leben ein.

Kuh und Kalb
im warmen Stall
rauchend im Abschiedsschweiss—
der goldgefasste Schrecken
des Schöpfungsbeginns
rückwärts
wurzelnd
in ihren Augen.

Awakening

Awakening—
Voices of birds
from the well of night
time counting with water—
evening-morning star
pale seed
sharp with thorn
strews death into life.

Cow and calf
in the warm stall
smoking in the sweat of parting—
the gold-set terror
of creation's beginning
rooting
backwards
in their eyes.

Sind Gräber Atempause für die Sehnsucht?
Leiseres Schaukeln an Sternenringen?
Agonie im Nachtschatten,
bevor die Trompeten blasen
zur Auffahrt für alle,
zum Leben verwesenden Samenkörner?

Leise, leise,
während die Würmer
die Gestirne der Augäpfel verzehren?

Are graves breath-space for longing?

Are graves breath-space for longing?
Swinging more gently on rings of stars?
Agony in shadow of night,
before the trumpets blow
for the ascension of all,
seeds rotting to life?

Gently, gently,
while the worms
devour the constellations of the eyeballs?

Hindurchsterben wie der Vogel die Luft
bis in die Waldseele
die sich im Veilchen verengt,
bis in die blutende Fischkieme
des Meeres End- und Leidensmusik—

Bis in das Landwerden
hinter der Wahnsinnsgrimasse
wo der Brunnen mit dem unterirdischen Ausgang
vielleicht hinter das Schmerzensbett
der Tränen führt.

To die through it like a bird through the air

To die through it like a bird through the air
even into the soul of the forest
that narrows in the violet,
even into the bleeding gill
of the sea's final and grieving music—

Even into the land becoming land
behind the grimace of madness
where the well with the subterranean outlet
perhaps leads behind
the painful bed of tears.

Hier unten aufgestellt
Kriegsgeräte, nachtgefärbt
unter dem Sternbild des Schützen,
Hieroglyphe grosser Bereitschaft.

Und getrennt Oben und Unten
von Geburts- und Todesmeilen
ohne unser Verständnis.

Aber die Sehnsuchtspfeile gespitzt
hüben und drüben
und die gleichen erzenen Köcher
als Bewahrer des Aufbruchs.

Machines of war set up

Machines of war set up
here below, night-stained
beneath Sagittarius,
hieroglyph of great preparedness.

And above and below divided
by miles of birth and death
without our understanding.

But the arrows of longing
sharpened by both sides
and the same iron quivers
as preservers of zero hour.

Haar, mein Haar

Haar, mein Haar,
ausschlagend in knisternden Funken—
einer Wüste Ginsterstrauch,
erinnerungsentzündet.

Haar, mein Haar,
welcher Sonnenglutball
ist in deine Nacht
zur Ruhe gelegt worden?

In deinen Spitzen stirbt eine Welt!
Gott hat sie leise gebettet,
auslöschend
in einem tränendurchströmten Leib.

Aber auch
in einer Kindersehnsucht
reissendem Verlangen
nach seiner Feuerbälle
ewig wachsendem Beginn.

Hair, my hair

Hair, my hair,
erupting in crackling sparks—
gorse of a desert,
ignited by memory.

Hair, my hair,
what ball of fiery sun
has been laid to rest
in your night?

A world dies in your tips!
God bedded them softly,
extinguishing them
in a body swept through by tears.

But also
in the impetuous demand
of a child's longing
for the ever-growing beginning
of its balls of fire.

Wenn nicht dein Brunnen, Melusine

Wenn nicht dein Brunnen, Melusine,
aller Märchen zweiten Ausgang
im Herzeweh hätte,
längst wären wir
in die versteinte Auferstehung
einer Osterinsel eingegangen—

Aber wenn dein Echoangesicht,
mit der Müdigkeiten Akelei bestreut,
Sterben übt im Sabbatgold,
trinkt unser Blut Erinnerung
in einer Landschaft,
die schon da gewesen,
und in der schlummerleichten Vorgeburt
der Seele—

Melusine, if your well had not

Melusine, if your well had not
the second ending of all fairy tales
in its heartache,
we should long have passed away
in the petrified resurrection
of an Easter Island—

But when your echo-face,
strewn with the columbine of weariness,
rehearses dying in the gold of the Sabbath,
our blood drinks memory
in a landscape
which was there before,
and in the easy sleep
before the soul was born—

In der Morgendämmerung

In der Morgendämmerung,
wenn die traumbedruckte Münze der Nacht
gewendet wird
und Rippen, Haut, Augäpfel
zu ihrer Geburt gezogen sind—

der Hahn mit weissem Kamm kräht,
ist der furchtbare Augenblick
der gottlosen Armut da,
ein Kreuzweg erreicht—

Wahnsinn heisst des Königs Trommler—
gestilltes Blut fliesst—

In the dawn light

In the dawn light,
when the dream-minted coin of night
is turned
and ribs, skin, eyeballs
are drawn to their birth—

the cock with the white comb crows,
the terrible moment
of godless poverty is here,
a crossroad reached—

the king's drummer is named "Madness"—
stanched blood flows—

Chassidim Tanzen

Nacht weht
mit todentrissnen Fahnen

Schwarze Hüte
Gottes Blitz-Ableiter
rühren das Meer auf

wiegen es
wiegen es aus

werfen es an den Strand
dort wo das Licht
die schwarzen Wunden ausgeschnitten hat.

Auf der Zunge
wird die Welt geschmeckt
abgesungen
die atmet mit der Jenseitslunge.

Auf dem Sieben-Leuchter
beten die Plejaden—

Hasidim Dancing

Night flutters
with flags torn from death

Black hats
God's lightning rods
stir up the sea

weigh it
weight it out

cast it upon the shore
there where the light
has carved black wounds.

The world which breathes
with lungs of the beyond
is tasted on the tongue
chanted out.

The Pleiades pray
on the seven-branched candelabra—

Nicht nur Land ist Israel!

Nicht nur Land ist Israel!
Vom Durst in die Sehnsucht,
von der rotangeheizten Mitternachtswurzel
durch die Türen des Ackerkornes
zu den geisterblauen Hauchtrinkern
hinter der Gnade zuckender Blindenbinde.
Flügel der Prophetie
an der Schulter aus Wüstensand.
Deine Pulse im Nachtgewitter reitend,
die erzenen Füsse
deiner Ewigkeit-schnaubenden Berge
galoppierend
bis in der Kindergebete
milchweissem Schaum.

Deiner Fusspuren kreisende Meridiane
im Salz des Sündenfalls,
deine grüne Segenswurzel eingeschlummert
im gemarterten Himmel der Wüste,
die offene Gotteswunde
im Gefieder der Luft—

Israel is not only land!

Israel is not only land!
From thirst into longing,
from the red-heated midnight-root
through the doors of the field's seed
to the ghost-blue drinkers of breath
behind the grace of the twitching blindfold.
Wings of prophecy
by the shoulder of desert sand.
Riding your pulses in the night-storm,
the iron feet
of your eternity-snorting mountains
galloping
even in the milk-white foam
of children's prayers.

Circling meridians of your footprints
in the salt of original sin,
your green root of blessing fallen asleep
in the tortured desert sky,
the open wound of God
in the plumage of air—

Später Erstling!

Später Erstling!
Mit dem Spaten heimgekommen
ins Ungeschachtete,
Ungezimmerte,
nur in die Linie,
die läuft wieder
durch die Synagoge der Sehnsucht
von Tod in Geburt.

Dein Sand wieder,
deiner Wüste Goldmaske
vor der Engelskämpfe
heruntergebogenem Himmel,
vor den flammenden Früchten
deiner *Gott* sprechenden Nacht.

Später Erstling,
Rose aus Salz,
mit dem Schlaf der Geburten
wie eine dunkle Weinranke
hängend an deiner Schläfe . . .

Late firstborn!

Late firstborn!
You have come home with the spade
into the unexcavated,
the unconstructed,
but into the line
that leads again
through the synagogue of longing
from death into birth.

Again your sand,
golden mask of your desert
facing the bent-down sky
of angels' battles,
facing the flaming fruits
of your night which says *God.*

Late firstborn,
rose of salt,
with the sleep of births
like a dark tendril of vine
hanging at your brow . . .

Dieses Land

Dieses Land
ein Kern
darin eingeritzt

Sein Name!

Schlaf mit Sternenzähnen hält ihn fest
im harten Apfelfleisch der Erde
mit Psalmenknospen
klopft er Auferstehung an.

Dieses Land
und alle seine Pfade
umblüht blau
mit Zeitlos

alle Spuren laufen ausserhalb—

Sand vulkanisch zitternd
von Widderhörnern
aus dem Traum geschaufelt.

Prophetenstunde eilte schnell
die Toten aus der Leichenhaut zu schälen
wie des Löwenzahnes Samen
nur beflügelt mit Gebeten
fuhren sie nach Haus—

This land

This land
a kernel
on it carved

His name!

Star-toothed sleep holds him fast
in the hard apple-flesh of earth
with buds of psalms
he taps out resurrection.

This land
and all its paths
blossoming blue
with timelessness

all tracks run outside—

Sand trembling volcanically
shoveled from the dream
by rams' horns.

The hour of the prophets hastened
to peel the corpse-skin from the dead
like dandelion seed
but winged with prayer
they traveled home—

Immer noch Mitternacht auf diesem Stern
und die Heerscharen des Schlafes.
Nur einige von den grossen Verzweiflern
haben so geliebt,
dass der Nacht Granit aufsprang
vor ihres Blitzes weissschneidendem Geweih.

So Elia; wie ein Wald mit ausgerissenen Wurzeln
erhob er sich unter dem Wacholder,
schleifte, Aderlass eines Volkes,
blutige Sehnsuchtsstücke hinter sich her,
immer den Engelfinger
wie einen Müdigkeit ansaugenden Mondstrahl
an seine Schwere geheftet,
Untiefen heimwärtsziehend—

Und Christus! An der Inbrunst Kreuz
nur geneigtes Haupt—
den Unterkiefer hängend,
mit dem Felsen:
Genug.

Still midnight on this star

Still midnight on this star
and the hosts of sleep.
Only a few of the great despairers
have so loved
that the granite of night burst
before the white-cleaving antlers of their lightning.

Thus Elijah: like a forest with torn-out roots
he arose beneath the juniper,
dragged, bloodletting of a people,
bloody bits of longing behind him,
the angel's finger,
like a moon-ray which sucks weariness in,
always touching his weight,
drawing the shallows homewards—

And Christ! On the cross of passion
only a bowed head—
the jaw hanging,
with the rock:
Enough.

Daniel mit der Sternenzeichnung

Daniel mit der Sternenzeichnung
erhob sich aus den Steinen
in Israel.
Dort wo die Zeit heimisch wurde im Tod
erhob sich Daniel,
der hohen Engel Scherbeneinsammler,
Aufbewahrer des Abgerissenen,
verlorene Mitte zwischen Anfang und Ende
setzend.

Daniel, der die vergessenen Träume noch
hinter dem letzten Steinkohlenabhang hervorholt.

Daniel, der Belsazar Blut lesen lehrte,
diese Schrift verlorener Wundränder,
die in Brand gerieten.

Daniel, der das verweinte Labyrinth zwischen
Henker und Opfer durchwandert hat,

Daniel hebt seinen Finger
aus der Abendröte
in Israel.

Daniel with the mark of stars

Daniel with the mark of stars
arose out of the stones
in Israel.
There where time grew to be at home in death
Daniel arose,
the high angels' gatherer of fragments,
keeper of things torn down,
setting a lost center between beginning
and end.

Daniel who fetches forgotten dreams
even from behind the last slope of coal.

Daniel who taught Belshazzar to read blood,
this script of lost edges of wounds
which took fire.

Daniel who wandered through the tear-stained labyrinth
between hangman and victim,

Daniel lifts his finger
from the evening-red
in Israel.

Mutterwasser

Mutterwasser
Sintflut
die ins Salz zog—Gerippe aus Sterben—
Erinnerungsstein
gesetzt
unter des Mondes Silbertreppe
in Ur
da wo das Blut der Nachtwandlerschar
zu Chaldäa
stürzte
durch die blaue Ader der Finsternis.

Da liest der Ausgräber
in der Bibel des Staubes
eingeküsstes Muster
königlich Gewebtes
und
sieht die Kette
golden
den Staub sonnen.

Der Hals der traulich
zwischen dem Geschmeide einging
in seine Nachtexistenz
liess immer noch
nebelgraues Gedenken zurück.

Musizierende Gestirne
rauschten wie Wein
in Abram's Ohr

Maternal water

Maternal water
deluge
that soaked into salt—skeleton made of dying—
stone of memory
set
beneath the moon's silver stair
in Ur
there where the blood of the sleepwalking crowd
of Chaldea
fell
through the blue vein of darkness.

There the archaeologist
reads in the Bible of dust
kissed-in pattern
royal wove
and
sees the chain
light
the dust with gold.

The jeweled neck
which passed smugly
into its nocturnal existence
still leaves
a mist-gray memory behind.

Music-making constellations
roared like wine
in Abram's ear

bis er rückwärts stürzte
abgerissen
getroffen
von einem Tod
der kein Tod ist—

until he fell backwards
torn down
struck
by a death
that is no death—

Und klopfte mit dem Hammer seines Herzens
und riss des Todes Efeu fort von Bibelgräbern
und sah das Feuer- Wasser- Luft- und Sandgesicht entblösst
und sah das leere Meer von Stern zu Stern:
Die Einsamkeit; und sah in aller Augen Heimatwehe,
und alle Flügel hatten Heimat nur als Ort
und Abschied war ein Blatt vom Wort,

das fiel, und Seinen Namen hinterliess,
der wie ein Falke aus dem Sterben stiess—

And hammered with the beating of his heart

And hammered with the beating of his heart
and tore death's ivy from the Bible-graves
and saw stripped bare the fire- air- water- sand-face
and saw the empty sea from star to star:
The loneliness; saw all eyes long for home
and all wings had as homeland only place—
leaf of the word the last embrace,

the leaf that fell, leaving His Name behind,
which swooped from death, a falcon in the wind—

Und Metatron, der höchste aller Engel,
fünfhundert Meilen hoch,
und schlägt das Rad
aus Lichtgefieder und lässt Musik,
daran die Welten hängen, klingen,
der Liebe Inbegriff!

So tief misst Sehnsucht aus
der Worte Meer, bis das Gestrahle
aufbricht—und Leben hinnaht
mit dem Wundenmale—

And Metatron the highest of all angels,
five hundred miles in height,
and spreads his wings
of feathered light and lets the music sound
on which the worlds depend,
embodiment of love!

Thus deeply longing measures out
the sea of words, until the bright light
breaks— and with stigmata
life comes into sight—

Und aus der dunklen Glut ward Jakob angeschlagen

Und aus der dunklen Glut ward Jakob angeschlagen
und so verrenkt; so war's am ersten Abend eingezeichnet.
Was im Gebiss der Mitternacht geschah,
ist so mit schwarzem Rätselmoos verflochten—
es kehrt auch niemand heil zu seinem Gott zurück—

Doch die entgleisten Sterne ruhen aus im Anfangswort
und die verzogene Sehnsucht hinkt an ihren Ort.

Jacob was smitten out of dark conflagration

Jacob was smitten out of dark conflagration
and crippled thus; so in the first dusk it was written down.
What happened in the teeth of midnight
is so entwined with the black moss of riddle—
and no one goes back unscathed to his God—

But in the first word rest stars fallen from their orbit
and twisted longing limps towards the place it shall inhabit.

Die Stunde zu Endor

Niemand weiss um die runde Leere in der Luft,
die keines Mundes Rosenblatt ausfüllt.
Dein Geheimnis,
mein Geheimnis
und das aus Ewigkeit
einer unsichtbaren Sonne Goldtopas.

Wohin zieht unsere Wirklichkeit aus?
Wohin die Gewitter des Blutes,
ihre Astraladern suchend?

Und Samuel sprach Abgeschiedenes
in der Stunde zu Endor.

Im Schrecken der Zaubernacht
liegt Sauls Gebetsrubin vergraben,
aller Mordgedanken Rubin,
aller verrenkten Leidenschaft Edelstein.

Und die kreisende Dämonin,
Gefängnisse ziehend aus Luft,
bis über die Grenze sich biegt
das klare Gesicht.

Und Samuel nahm Sauls Totenmaske ab,
handlos im Schwarzen.
Nur ein Haar—funkengeleckt—
soll übrigbleiben
vor David, dem Ewigkeitsblitz.

The Hour at Endor

No one knows of the round void in the air
which no mouth's rose petal fills.
Your secret,
my secret
and that of eternity
gold topaz of an invisible sun.

To where does our reality depart?
Whither the storms of blood,
seeking their astral veins?

And Samuel spoke words of death
in the hour at Endor.

In the terror of the magic night
Saul's ruby of prayer lies buried,
ruby of all thoughts of murder,
all jewels of twisted passion.

And the circling witch,
tugging prisons of air,
until the clear face
bends across the border.

And Samuel took off Saul's death mask,
without hands in the darkness.
Only a hair—licked by sparks—
shall survive
before David, the lightning of eternity.

O, o überall Herde der Unrast todentzündet,
unsere Hinterlassenschaft an diesem Stern!
Gott, unser Entlarver, lässt sie schwelen
da und dort in der Verschwiegenheit.

Träume tragen Gewissenskleider,
Prophezeiungen in der Maske der Nacht.

Saul, der Jäger aus Schwermut,
verzehrt unter der schwarzen Angst-Feuer-Dornen-Krone,
will die Welt mit Fingern fangen,
aller Horizonte Rätselrinde zerbeissen,
den Knaben aus Sternmusik töten.

O die Stunde zu Endor!
Bezeugung der gekrümmten Jägerqual,
wo die Wunde der Begierde ihren Arzt findet,
aber nicht heilt—

Heimliches Land,
nur aus Begegnungen mit den Toten geschaffen,
nur aus Atem bewegtes—

Rune der Sehnsucht,
Hahnenschrei des Verrats,
der Quelle urreine Wanderung durstgetrübt—
Wahnsinnige werden aus dem Zenit deiner Stille geboren,
sind geduldlos geworden
aus Heimweh—

Niemand weiss, ob der Weltenraum blutet
mit blitzenden Stigmata
an seiner unsterblichen Not

O, O everywhere centers of unrest inflamed with death,
the estate we leave behind upon this star!
God, our unmasker, lets it smolder
here and there in secrecy.

Dreams wear clothes of conscience,
Prophecies in the mask of night.

Saul, hunting because of melancholy,
consumed under the black fear-fire-thorn-crown,
wants to catch the world with his fingers,
bite through the riddle-rind of all horizons,
kill the boy whose music is the stars.

O the hour at Endor!
Attestation of the twisted hunter's torment,
where the wound of desire finds its physician
but does not heal—

Secret land,
only created from encounters with the dead,
only moved by breath—

Rune of longing,
cockcrow of betrayal,
contaminated by thirst the spring's pure flow—
Madmen are born from the zenith of your silence,
have grown impatient
in their longing for home—

No one knows if the universe bleeds
with lightning stigmata
from its immortal need

und das Herz zu Tode drückt,
jedes Herz zu Tode drückt.

Kranker König!
Umstellt von der Steine Totenmusik,
Tanzmaske flatternder Schatten im Blute.

Hingegeben an den Mond der Harfe,
Fliehender, verfolgt zu Gott!

Aus der Fruchtschale der Welt
griffst du die Tollkirsche,
die alle Himmel falsch anfärbt
Blut-Krause-Minze sät.

Deine Pulse, klirrend im Jagedurst,
alle Verfolger haben in deinen Augen
ihr Lager aufgeschlagen—
dein Opfer rinnt in keiner Träne aus.

Die Zauberin in der Küche,
die geheime Flüsterin,
mit den Pupillen toter Fische würfelnd,
diesen weissen Blindensteinen
aus Gott-Ferne geformt.

Sie unterbläst die Welt
mit dem schneidenden Hauch ihres Mundes:
die Sternkathedrale,
wurzelenthoben, stürzt auf die Knie,
Zeitsand in der Wüste
falschem Sonnenanbetergesicht.

and chokes the heart to death,
chokes each heart to death.

Sick king!
surrounded by the stone's death-music,
dance mask of fluttering shadows in the blood.

Surrendered to the moon of the harp,
Fugitive, pursued to God!

Out of the world's fruit bowl
you seized the deadly nightshade,
which stains all skies the wrong color
sowing blood-curly-mint,

Your pulses, ringing with the hunter's passion,
all pursuers have set up
their camp in your eyes—
no tear flows for your victim.

The witch in the kitchen,
the secret whisperer,
dicing with the pupils of dead fish,
these white blindstones
formed from god-distance.

She blows beneath the world
with the cutting breath of her mouth:
the cathedral of stars,
released from its roots, falls to its knees,
time of sand in the desert's
deceitful sun-worshipping face.

Im schrecklichen Sturz aus Licht,
im Rosenquarz der Fleischvernichtung
Samuel kreist,
gewitternde Erinnerung—

O Saul—Gott-entlassen—

O beunruhigte Nacht,
Cherubim im zerfetzten Schwarzgefieder
diamantenbrennend—

Gerippe des Todes mit feurigen Wünschelruten,
königlichen Purpur schlagend.
Fledermäuse aus den Augenhöhlen,
Wahrsager im Atemzug der Luft,
Grabschrift im Schwefel der Morgendämmerung.

Horch die Stunde zu Endor!

Der kämpfenden Seele Sterbezelle!

Aufgerissen ist die Zeit,
diese Wunde vor Gott!

Angerührt ist der Wurm,
der gräbt lautlos das Ende—

O, o Musik aus zerfallenden Gerippen,
Finger an den opalnen Geräten des Sterbens
und der Meere geburtenverhüllter Schlaf—

In the terrible fall from light,
in the rose-quartz flesh-destruction,
Samuel circles,
stormy memory—

O Saul—dismissed by God—

O troubled night,
cherubim in the ragged black plumage
burning with diamonds—

Skeleton of death with fiery magic wands,
striking royal purple.
Bats from the eye sockets,
soothsayer in the breath of air,
epitaph in the sulphur of dawn.

Hear the hour at Endor!

Death cell of the fighting soul!

Time is torn open,
this wound before God!

The worm is touched
which silently digs the end—

O, O music from disintegrating skeletons,
finger on the opal instruments of dying
and the seas' birth-veiled sleep—

Jonathan, selig gezeichnet
in Davids Liebesgewölk,
Arche der Abgeschiedenen,
im steinkohlenstarren Nachtgeschlecht verborgen—

Wind der Erlösung—

Auf der Sternenwaage gewogen
wiegt des Leidens
flammengekrümmter Wurm
Gott aus—

Jonathan drawn blissfully
in David's cloud of love,
Ark of the dead and gone,
hidden in the coal-rigid race of night—

Wind of redemption—

Weighed on the scale of stars
the flame-bent worm
of suffering
weighs out God—

Nachdem du aufbrachst

Nachdem du aufbrachst
Loch des Schweigens gähnt
Grab—darin einer Nachtwache Wandlung
schon ohne Ränder
Kuss in die Anfänge—

Die Welt aus deinen Augen fiel
Blind-Ball
rollend
in das Muschelnest der Zeit—

Unter dem Wasser spricht jemand deine Musik
im Luftzug wird Neues gemessen—

kopflose Schatten stürzen
zur Nachtversammlung.

Verschlossenes wetterleuchtet
durch die Tür

weisser Zügel
aus ungesprochenem Wortgespann.

Now you have gone forth

Now you have gone forth
hole of silence yawns
grave—in it a vigil's transformation
already without edges
a kiss into the beginnings—

The world fell out of your eyes
blind-ball
rolling into the seashell nest of time—

Beneath the water someone speaks your music
in the draught something new is measured—

headless shadows rush
to the nightly assembly.

What is locked up shines through the door
like sheet lightning

white rein
made of unspoken words in harness.

Was stieg aus deines Leibes weissen Blättern

Was stieg aus deines Leibes weissen Blättern
die ich dich vor dem letzten Atemzug
noch Mutter nannte?

Was liegt auf dem Leinen für Sehnsuchtsverlassenes?

Welche Wunde schliesst die durchschmerzte Zeit
die rann aus deinem Puls
mit Sternmusik?

Wohin der Kranz deiner warmen Umarmung?
In welchen Azur dein geflüsterter Segen?

Welches Lächeln gebar sich
an deines Fingers
luftiger Zeichensprache?

Auf welchen Spuren
soll ich deines Blutes Dichtung suchen?
Wo deine Seligkeit anfragen?

Wie unter meinen Füssen
die saugende Kugel fortstossen
um die Todestreppe hinaufzustürmen?

Oft waren wir
geladen
zu überzeitlichen Empfängen
versteinerte Rinden
Meer- und Feuer-Vorhänge zurückschlagend—

What rose out of the white leaves of your body

What rose out of the white leaves of your body
You whom before your last breath
I still called mother?

What kind of longing-forsaken thing lies on the linen sheet?

What wound closes the suffered time
which ran out of your pulse
with starry music?

Where is the wreath of your warm embrace?
In which azure your whispered blessing?

What smile was born
at the airy sign-language
of your finger?

On which track
shall I seek the poetry of your blood?
Where inquire for your salvation?

How push away
the sucking ball from under my feet
to storm up the stair of death?

We were often
invited
to time-transcending receptions
petrified bark
pushing back curtains of sea and fire—

Aber nun:
die Entlassene der Liebe hier
gebeugt über das Leid-Steine-Trauerspiel
dem Haar der Trennung nachsinnend

und eine Herzenszeit schaffend
wo Tod sich atmend füllt
und wieder abnimmt—

But now:
the woman love dismissed bent
here over the sorrow-stone-tragedy
musing on the hair of separation

and creating a time of the heart
where death breathing fills itself
and again diminishes—

Nur im Schlaf haben Sterne Herzen

Nur im Schlaf haben Sterne Herzen
und Münder.
Ebbe- und Flut-Atem
üben mit den Seelen
die letzte Vorbereitung.
Und die Felsen, die aus dem Nassen steigen,
die schweren Albgesichter,
sind doch
vom Stemmeisen der Sehnsucht durchbohrte
brennende Walfische—
Wie aber wird Liebe sein
am Ende der Nächte,
bei den durchsichtig gewordenen Gestirnen?
Denn Erz kann nicht mehr Erz sein,
wo Selige sind—

Stars have hearts and mouths

Stars have hearts and mouths
only in sleep.
Ebb and flow of breathing
rehearses with souls
the last preparation.
And yet the rocks, which climb from the wet,
the heavy nightmare faces,
are burning whales
pierced by crowbars of longing—
But how will love be
at the end of the nights,
beside the constellations which have grown transparent?
For iron can be iron no more
where the blessed are—

Wie aber

Wie aber,
wenn Eines schon hier
mit Augen umfasst
fliegende Steine,
die Goldenes gebären,
Feuerzähne,
die Dunkel fortkauen,
und die taubstumme Schrift
aus Abendblut—

Schweigen über dem verblassenden
Sternbild der Worte—

einatmend des Todes
dunkles Gewürz,

und im rosa Licht der Fallsüchtigen
aufblättert Meerzwiebelhimmel?

Wie erst dann,
losgelassen alle Geländer,
in der Verheissung Falltuch springend,
unter der Füsse schwebender Fanfare

der verlorene Sand der Zeit—

But how

But how,
if something already here
holds in view
flying stones
which give birth to what is golden,
teeth of fire
which chew away the dark,
and the deaf-dumb script
of evening blood—

Silence above the paling
constellation of words—

inhaling death's
dark spice,

and peels off the quillitic sky
in the pink light of epileptics?

How only then,
all railings let go,
leaping into the fire net of the promise,
under the swaying fanfare of the feet

the lost sand of time—

Alles weisst du unendlich nun

Alles weisst du unendlich nun,
o meine Mutter—
auch die Stelle, wo den Propheten
das Ende des Weges
flammend vom Leibe gerissen wurde.

Auch des Esau
ins Fell der Niederlage
geweinte Träne.

Auch die Nebelknospe
der Schwermut im Blute.

Alles weisst du unendlich nun,
o meine Mutter—
auch der Träume und Zeichen
zerfetzte Milchstrassenwunder.

Auch deiner offenen Atemwunde
Entlassenes!

Alles weisst du unendlich nun,
o meine Mutter—
denn Rahels Grab ist längst Musik geworden—
und Stein und Sand
ein Atemzug im Meer,
und Wiegenlied von aller Sterne:
Auf- im Untergang—

Und Ränder überall aus Meer—

du weisst—

O my mother

O my mother,
now you know everything unendingly—
know too the place where the end of the way
was torn in flames
from the prophets' bodies.

And Esau's tear
wept into
the hide of defeat.

And the mist-bud
of melancholy in the blood.

O my mother,
now you know everything unendingly—
know too the Milky Way's ragged wonders
of dreams and signs.

And what is released
from the open wound of your breath!

O my mother,
now you know everything unendingly—
for Rachel's grave has long since turned to music—
and stone and sand
a breath in the sea,
and cradle song from all the stars:
rise in the fall—

And borders everywhere of sea—

you know—

Dornengekrönt

Hieronymus Bosch

Immer wieder
durch einen verhexten Handgriff
den Nabel der Liebe gesprengt.
Immer wieder
der Folterer über schwanengebogenem Rücken
die Geissel lange schon im Traume erprobt.

Immer wieder
die zerpeitschte Aura
über dem entblätterten Leib.

Immer wieder
die Sehnsucht, aller Gräber Frühlingsknospe
mit dem Steinzeitfinger zur Träne zerdrückt.

Immer wieder
die Blutschlange züngelnd
im Hautwams der Henker.

Immer wieder
die Blicke des Opfers zugedeckt
mit Gott—Auszug—Asche—

Thorncrowned

Hieronymus Bosch

Again and again
the navel of love exploded
by a bewitched twist of the hand.
Again and again
the torturer above the swan-bent back
the scourge long since tried out in dream.

Again and again
the lashed aura
above the peeled body.

Again and again
the longing, spring bud of all graves,
crushed to a tear by the stone-age finger.

Again and again
the snake of blood hissing
in the skin jerkins of hangmen.

Again and again
the victim's glances covered
with God—Exodus—ashes—

Hinterm Augenlid

Hinterm Augenlid
blaue Adern
am Mondstein der Zeit,
Hahnenschrei
öffnet die Wunde
am Haupt des Propheten.

In Spiralen
lodern Arme—Beine
verblühen ausserhalb,
aber der Leib sinkt,
Staubfrucht,
mit eisigem Samen
für tödlichen Gebrauch.

Behind the eyelid

Behind the eyelid
blue veins
on the moonstone of time,
cockcrow
opens the wound
on the prophet's head.

Arms flame
in spirals—legs
wither outside,
but the body sinks,
fruit of dust,
with icy seed
for deathly use.

Welcher Stoff

Welcher Stoff,
welcher Nebel,
welche geheimen Geburten
aus den Gräbern
mit dem Zickzack-Blitz
der verstossnen Wünsche aufsteigend,

malend unterm Augenlid-Perlmutter—

Der Weltenraum knospend im Fiebergestirn
versunkene Blutkapellen
läutendes Pompeji—

Schneeflocken des Heimwehs,
schmelzend im Winterschlaf.

Welche Nächte, welche Sterne
in den Adern versteckt,
welch flötender Hirtenknabe
auf den Weiden des Meeres—

Verkohlte Geheimnisse,
mit schwachem Atem angeblasen

Die Ferne zusammengerollt im Mond,
einer weissen Kastanie
dornenbespicktes Gebet—

What substance

What substance,
what mist,
what secret births
rising from the graves
with the zigzag lightning
of disowned wishes,

painting under eyelid mother-of-pearl—

Space budding in fever constellations
sunk chapels of blood
tolling Pompeia—

Snowflakes of homesickness,
melting in winter sleep.

What nights, what stars
hidden in the veins,
what fluting shepherd boy
on the pastures of the sea—

Charred secrets,
kindled with weak breath

Distance furled in the moon,
a white chestnut
of thorn-studded prayer—

Welche Todesarbeit,
Käfer auf den Rücken gelegt,
der Füsse letzten Krampf
in Schweigen vereist,

Bis die Schleuse hochgezogen wird
mit der Überschwemmung aus Sterben,

mit den morgenbrennenden Armen
aus Wiedersehn—

What work of death,
beetles turned on their backs,
the foot's last cramp
frozen in silence,

Until the sluice is opened
for the flood from dying,

with the dawn-burning arms
of meeting once more—

Das wirft die Nabelschnur

Das wirft die Nabelschnur
an die Wand des Tempels
vom blutigen Gischt der Geburt
zum Gischt der blauverwesenden Koralle
des Todseins.

O wie tobt die Stille
auf der Bergeslinie—

Tibet ist ein Strahl,
magisch eingekerbt die Gotteswunde,
die reicht für alle Abende
über den Schmerzensländern.

Hier aber
in den Verleugnungen
zwischen Drache und Schlange,
anderswo
vielleicht stossend im Widdergehörn
oder aber
auf der Strasse im Verladen des Kalbes.

Zu Ende geküsst ist die Welt—

Botschaft bewegt sich im Sand,
will auferstehn

Schwarzmond reisst Türen auf,
reisefertig ist der Stern,
betet mit den Wellen.

This casts the navel cord

This casts the navel cord
on the wall of the temple
from the bloody foam of birth
to the foam of death's
rotting blue coral.

Oh, how the stillness
rages on the line of hills—

Tibet is a beam of light,
magically notched into God's wound,
which suffices for all evenings
above the lands of pain.

But here
in the denials
between dragon and snake,
somewhere else
thrusting perhaps in the ram's horns
or perhaps
in the street where the calf is loaded.

The world is kissed to its end—

The message moves in the sand,
seeks resurrection

Black moon tears open doors,
the star is ready for the journey,
prays with the waves.

Im blauen Kristall

Im blauen Kristall
die Zeit wartet
auf die betäubte Sehnsucht,
die ihren Raum durchschmerzen muss—

Die Sehnsucht,
diese gefangene Sternbedrängerin,
abgebröckelte
aus namenlosen Frühlingen,
misst wieder
mein Leid im Puls,
die rasende Reiterin
in übernächtiges Land—

Im Sande fährt sie mit mir
im heimwärtsziehenden
Segel der Melancholie,
Nachtveilchen
verstreuten
dem gekreuzigten Fisch
in der versteinerten Träne
aus Vergessenheit—

Time waits

Time waits
in the blue crystal
for the numbed longing
which must suffer through its space—

The longing,
this captive stormer of stars,
crumbled
out of nameless springs,
takes the pulse
of my pain again,
the furious rider
into the sleepless land—

It travels with me in the sand
in the homeward-seeking
sail of melancholy,
night violets
strewed
the crucified fish
in the petrified tear
from oblivion—

Und der Perlpunkt der Ewigkeit

Und der Perlpunkt der Ewigkeit
wieder in Muscheln versteckt,
und die Hieroglyphe des Lichtes
wieder im Auge
tränenversprechend,

und der Sterne himmlische Strategie
wieder ruhelos
aus der Ewigkeitsübung gerissen,
schreiend mit Meteoren,
die auf Geschwisterstrassen landen
mit dem gleichen Musikstück aus Blei
und Vergessenheitsasche.

Aber Ausflüge
höher als Tod
kehren nicht in Krankenstuben zurück,
diese Vögel nisten weiter
in ihrer eigenen Freude.

And the pearly point of eternity

And the pearly point of eternity
hidden again in seashells,
and the hieroglyph of light
again in the eye
promising tears,

and the stars' heavenly strategy
again torn
restlessly from the exercise of eternity,
screaming with meteors
which land on sister streets
with the same piece of music made of lead
and oblivion's ashes.

But excursions
higher than death
do not return to sickrooms,
these birds continue to nest
in their own joy.

Ich habe dich wiedergesehn

Ich habe dich wiedergesehn,
Rauch hat dich gezeichnet,
den Mantel der Verpuppung
aus sterbender Substanz
warfst du ab,
eine untergegangene Sonne,
am Faden deiner Liebe
leuchtete die Nacht auf,
die sich hob
wie einer Schwalbenschwinge
vorgefalteter Flug.
Ich habe einen Halm des Windes gefasst,
eine Sternschnuppe hing daran—

I saw you again

I saw you again,
smoke had marked you,
you cast off the cloak
of the chrysalis
made of dying substance,
a sun that had sunk
on the thread of your love
lit the night
which rose
like the folded flight
of a swallow's wing.
I grasped a blade of the wind,
a shooting star hung from it—

Hier

Hier—
wo ich scheiterte im Salz,
hier am Meer
mit seinen blauen Säuglingen,
die sich nähren
mondbesessen
an der Seelenamme
hier im Sand,
der im Tierkreis getanzt
und wieder
mit Ungeborenem verschlüsselt liegt

erscheinst du
rückwärts
in der verdunkelten Leere,
die wartend um dich steht,
ein Korb gefüllt zu werden

mit Früchten,
die auf metallenen Gestirnstrassen fahren
oder
in der Liebe Zugluft
verfrachtet werden—

meinen Atem reiche ich dir
und falle ab,
wieder auf einer Distel zu wohnen,
die niemals Blume wird—

Here

Here—
in the salt where I failed,
here by the sea
with its blue sucklings
which feed
moon-obsessed
on the wet-nurse of souls
here in the sand,
that danced in the zodiac
and lies again
enciphered with what is unborn

you appear
backwards
in the darkened void,
which stands waiting around you,
a basket to be filled

with fruit
which travels on metal roads of stars
or
is shipped
in the draught of love—

I give you my breath
and fall,
to dwell again on a thistle
which will never flower—

Von Nacht gesteinigt

Von Nacht gesteinigt,
hob mich Schlaf
in Landsflucht weit hinaus

Grenzlinien
die Geburt
an meiner Haut gezogen einst
verlöschte Tod
mit einer Hand Musik

Erlöste Liebe
sich ihr Sternbild
in die Freiheit schrieb—

Stoned by night

Stoned by night,
sleep lifted me
far away into exile

Borderlines
which birth
once drew on my skin
death obliterated
with a hand of music

Love redeemed
inscribed its constellation
into freedom—

Flight and Metamorphosis

Translated by Ruth and Matthew Mead

Dies ist der dunkle Atem

Dies ist der dunkle Atem
von Sodom
und die Last
von Ninive
abgelegt
an der offenen Wunde
unserer Tür.

Dies ist die heilige Schrift
in Landsflucht
in den Himmel kletternd
mit allen Buchstaben,
die befiederte Seligkeit
in einer Honigwabe bergend.

Dies ist der schwarze Laokoon
an unser Augenlid geworfen
durchlöchernd Jahrtausende
der verrenkte Schmerzensbaum
spriessend in unserer Pupille.

Dies sind salzerstarrte Finger
tränentropfend im Gebet.

Dies ist Seine Meeresschleppe
zurückgezogen
in die rauschende Kapsel der Geheimnisse.

Dies ist unsere Ebbe
Wehegestirn
aus unserem zerfallenden Sand—

This is the dark breath

This is the dark breath
of Sodom
and the burden
of Nineveh
laid down
at the open wound
of our door.

This is the holy scripture
in exile
climbing into the sky
with every letter,
hiding the plumed bliss
in a honeycomb.

This is the black Laocoön
cast upon our eyelid
piercing millennia
the twisted tree of pain
sprouting in our pupil.

These are salt-numbed fingers
shedding tears in prayer.

This is His oceanic train
withdrawn
into the roaring capsule of mysteries.

This is our ebb
star of woe
out of our crumbling sand—

Wie leicht

Wie leicht
wird Erde sein
nur eine Wolke Abendliebe
wenn als Musik erlöst
der Stein in Landsflucht zieht

und Felsen die
als Alp gehockt
auf Menschenbrust
Schwermutgewichte
aus den Adern sprengen.

Wie leicht
wird Erde sein
nur eine Wolke Abendliebe
wenn schwarzgeheizte Rache
vom Todesengel magnetisch
angezogen
an seinem Schneerock
kalt und still verendet.

Wie leicht
wird Erde sein
nur eine Wolke Abendliebe
wenn Sternenhaftes schwand
mit einem Rosenkuss
aus Nichts—

How light

How light
earth will be
only a cloud of evening love
when released as music
the stone goes into exile

and rocks which
squatted like nightmares
on human breasts
blast burdens of melancholy
from the veins.

How light
earth will be
only a cloud of evening love
when black-hot revenge
attracted magnetically
by the angel of death
perishes cold and silent
at his cloak of snow.

How light
earth will be
only a cloud of evening love
when all that is starlike vanishes
with a kiss of roses
out of the void—

Jäger

Jäger
mein Sternbild
zielt
in heimlichen Blutpunkt: Unruhe . . .
und der Schritt asyllos fliegt—

Aber der Wind ist kein Haus
leckt nur wie Tiere
die Wunden am Leib—

Wie nur soll man die Zeit
aus den goldenen Fäden der Sonne ziehen?
Aufwickeln
für den Kokon des Seidenschmetterlings
Nacht?

O Dunkelheit
breite aus deine Gesandtschaft
für einen Wimpernschlag:

Ruhe auf der Flucht.

Hunter

Hunter
my constellation
aims
at secret blood-point: Unrest . . .
and the step without refuge flies—

But the wind is not a house
only licks like animals
the body's wounds—

But how shall time be drawn
from the golden threads of the sun?
Wound
for the cocoon of the silken butterfly
night?

O darkness
spread your mission
for a moment:

Rest during flight.

So weit ins Freie gebettet

So weit ins Freie gebettet
im Schlaf.
Landsflüchtig
mit dem schweren Gepäck der Liebe.

Eine Schmetterlingszone der Träume
wie einen Sonnenschirm
der Wahrheit vorgehalten.

Nacht
Nacht
Schlafgewand Leib
streckt seine Leere
während der Raum davonwächst
vom Staub ohne Gesang.

Meer
mit weissagenden Gischtzungen
rollt
über das Todeslaken
bis Sonne wieder sät
den Strahlenschmerz der Sekunde.

Bedded so far out in the open

Bedded so far out in the open
in sleep.
Fleeing the land
with the heavy burden of love.

A butterfly zone of dreams
held against truth
like a sunshade.

Night
night
nightgown body
stretches its emptiness
while space grows away
from dust without song.

Sea
with prophetic tongues of foam
rolls
over the shroud
until sun sows again
the second's radiant pain.

Heilige Minute

Heilige Minute
erfüllt vom Abschied
vom Geliebtesten
Minute
darin das Weltall
seine unlesbaren Wurzeln schlägt
vereint
mit der Vögel blindfliegender Geometrie
der Würmer Pentagramma
die nachtangrabenden

mit dem Widder
der auf seinem Echobild weidet
und der Fische Auferstehung
nach Mittwinter.

Einäugig zwinkert
und Herz verbrennend
die Sonne
mit der Löwentatze in der Spindel
zieht sie das Netz um die
Leidenden
dichter und dichter

denn nicht darf man wecken eines
wenn die Seele aushäusig ist

und seefahrend
vor Sehnsucht
sonst stirbt der Leib
verlassen
in der Winde verlorenem Gesicht.

Holy moment

Holy moment
filled with parting
from the one loved most
Moment
in which the universe
strikes its indecipherable roots
united
with the birds' blind-flying geometry
the pentagram of worms
which dig into the night

with the ram
which pastures on its echo-image
and the resurrection of fish
after midwinter.

The sun
twinkles one-eyed
burning the heart
with the lion's paw on the spindle
it draws the net
closer and closer
around sufferers

for no one may be woken
when the soul is elsewhere

and voyaging
in longing
or else the body will die
forsaken
in the wind's lost face.

263

Kind

Kind
Kind
im Orkan des Abschieds
stossend mit der Zehen weissflammendem Gischt
gegen den brennenden Horizontenring
suchend den geheimen Ausweg des Todes.

Schon ohne Stimme—ausatmend Rauch—

Liegend wie das Meer
nur mit Tiefe darunter
reissend an der Vertauung
mit den Springwogen der Sehnsucht—

Kind
Kind
mit der Grablegung deines Hauptes
der Träume Samenkapsel
schwer geworden
in endlicher Ergebung
bereit anderes Land zu besäen.

Mit Augen
umgedreht zum Muttergrund—

Du
in der Kerbe des Jahrhunderts gewiegt
wo Zeit mit gesträubten Flügeln
fassungslos ertrinkt
in der Überschwemmung
deines masslosen Untergangs.

Child

Child
Child
in the hurricane of parting
kicking with the toe's white-flaming foam
against the burning ring of the horizon
seeking the secret exit of death.

Already without a voice—breathing out smoke—

Lying like the sea
but with depth beneath it
tearing at the mooring
with the spring-tide of desire—

Child
Child
with the interment of your head
the seed pod of dreams
grown heavy
in final submission
ready to sow another land.

With eyes
turned to maternal soil—

You
cradled in the notch of the century
where time with ruffled wings
drowns bewildered
in the flood
of your endless doom.

Zwischen

Zwischen
deinen Augenbrauen
steht deine Herkunft
eine Chiffre
aus der Vergessenheit des Sandes.

Du hast das Meerzeichen
hingebogen
verrenkt
im Schraubstock der Sehnsucht.

Du säst dich mit allen Sekundenkörnern
in das Unerhörte.

Die Auferstehungen
deiner unsichtbaren Frühlinge
sind in Tränen gebadet.

Der Himmel übt an dir
Zerbrechen.

Du bist in der Gnade.

Your origin

Your origin
is set
between your eyebrows
a cipher
out of the sand's oblivion.

You have bent
the sign of the sea
twisted
in the vise of longing.

You sow yourself with the grain of each second
into the undreamed-of.

The resurrections
of your invisible springs
are bathed in tears.

On you the sky practices
its breaking.

You are in grace.

Aber vielleicht

Aber vielleicht
haben wir
vor Irrtum Rauchende
doch ein wanderndes Weltall geschaffen
mit der Sprache des Atems?

Immer wieder die Fanfare
des Anfangs geblasen
das Sandkorn in Windeseile geprägt
bevor es wieder Licht ward
über der Geburtenknospe
des Embryos?

Und sind immer wieder
eingekreist
in deinen Bezirken
auch wenn wir nicht der Nacht gedenken
und der Tiefe des Meeres
mit Zähnen abbeissen
der Worte Sterngeäder.

Und bestellen doch deinen Acker
hinter dem Rücken des Todes.

Vielleicht sind die Umwege des Sündenfalles
wie der Meteore heimliche Fahnenfluchten
doch im Alphabet der Gewitter
eingezeichnet neben den Regenbögen—

But perhaps

But perhaps
we
smoky with error
have still created a wandering universe
with the language of breath?

Again and again the fanfare
of beginning blown
the grain of sand coined at full speed
before it grew light again
above the embryo's
bud of birth?

And are again and again
encircled
in your domains
even when we do not remember night
and bite off with our teeth
the starry veins of words
from the depth of the sea.

And yet till your acre
behind the back of death.

Perhaps the detours of the Fall
are like meteors' secret desertions
but inscribed in the alphabet of storms
beside the rainbows—

Wer weiss auch
die Grade des Fruchtbarmachens
und wie die Saaten gebogen werden
aus fortgezehrten Erdreichen
für die saugenden Münder
des Lichts.

But who knows
the degrees of making fertile
and how the green corn is bent
from soils eaten away
for the sucking mouths
of light.

Im Alter

Im Alter
der Leib wird umwickelt
mit Blindenbinden
bis er kreist
hilflos
in Sonnenfinsternis.

Aber tief
im Meeresgang
Unruhe hebt
und senkt sich
in den gekreuzten Flügeln.

Tod
kaum gereift
ist schon neu befruchtet
aus Gräbern
das Öl der Heiligkeit gezogen.

Gestirne
in der Auferstehung
brennen Dunkelheit an.

Wieder ist Gott reisefertig.

In age

In age
the body is swathed
with blindfolds
until it circles
helplessly
in the sun's eclipse.

But deep
in the sway of the sea
unrest lifts
and sinks
in the crossed wings.

Death
hardly ripe
is already newly fructified
the oil of holiness drawn
out of graves.

Stars
in the resurrection
set fire to darkness.

God is ready again for the journey.

Uneinnehmbar

Uneinnehmbar
ist eure nur aus Segen errichtete
Festung
ihr Toten.

Nicht mit meinem Munde
der
Erde
Sonne
Frühling
Schweigen
auf der Zunge wachsen lässt
weiss ich das Licht
eures entschwundenen Alphabetes
zu entzünden.

Auch nicht
mit meinen Augen
darin Schöpfung einzieht
wie Schnittblumen
die von magischer Wurzel
alle Weissagung vergassen.

So muss ich denn aufstehen
und diesen Felsen durchschmerzen
bis ich Staubgeworfene
bräutlich Verschleierte
den Seeleneingang fand
wo das immer knospende Samenkorn
die erste Wunde
ins Geheimnis schlägt.

Impregnable

Impregnable
is your fortress
built only of blessing
you dead.

Not with my mouth
which lets
earth
sun
spring
silence
grow on the tongue
I know how to ignite
the light
of your vanished alphabet.

Nor
with my eyes
which creation enters
like cut flowers
which forgot all prophecy
of the magic root.

So then I must rise
and suffer through this rock
until, dust cast,
nuptially veiled,
I found entrance to the soul
where the ever-budding seed
strikes the first wound
into the mystery.

David

David
erwählt
noch in der Sünde
wie Springflut tanzend
gebogen
in heimlichen Mondphasen
vor der Bundeslade
losgerissene Erdwurzel
Heimwehgischt.

Aber
im Flammentopf der Erde
mit Pflanze und Getier
die Lenden hinauf
standen noch die Propheten
sahen aber schon
durch Gestein
hin zu Gott.

Christus nahm ab
an Feuer
Erde
Wasser
baute aus Luft
noch einen Schrei
und das
Licht
im schwarzumrätselten Laub
der einsamsten Stunde
wurde ein Auge
und sah.

David

David
chosen
even in sin
like spring-tide dancing
curved
in secret phases of the moon
before the ark of the covenant
root of earth torn loose
foam of homesickness.

But
in the flaming vessel of the earth
up to the thighs
in plant and beast
the prophets still stood
but already saw
through stone
to God.

Christ decreased
in fire
earth
water
but still built
a cry from air
and the light
in the foliage
surrounded by black riddles
of the loneliest hour
became an eye
and saw.

Gerettet

Gerettet
fällt vieles
in die Körbe der Erinnerungen
denn
auch dieses Nachtalter
wird seine Fossile haben
die schwarz geränderten Trauerschriften
seines schief gewachsenen Staubes.

Vielleicht
auch werden unsere nachgelassenen
Himmel
diese blassblauen Steine
heilende Magie üben
in andere Höllen niedergelegt

wird
dein Sterbegespräch
im Wehe-Wind
dem kalten Gespann der
sich streckenden Glieder
Zeiten durchatmen
und
glasbläserhaft biegen
verschwundene Liebesform

für den Mund eines Gottes—

Rescued

Rescued
much falls
into the baskets of memories
for
this night-age also
will have its fossils
the black-bordered mourning scripts
of its crookedly grown dust.

Perhaps
our posthumous skies
these pale blue stones
will also
practice healing magic
laid down in other hells

your dying words
in the wind of woe
the cold team
of the stretching limbs
will
breathe through ages
and
shape like a glassblower
a vanished form of love

for the mouth of a God—

So ist's gesagt

So ist's gesagt—
mit Schlangenlinien aufgezeichnet

Absturz.

Die Sonne
chinesisch Mandala
heilig verzogener Schmuck
zurück in innere Phasen heimgekehrt
starres Lächeln
fortgebetet
Lichtdrachen
zeitanspeiend
Schildträger war die Fallfrucht Erde
einst
goldangegleist—

Weissagungen
mit Flammenfingern zeigen:

Dies ist der Stern
geschält bis auf den Tod—

Dies ist des Apfels Kerngehäuse
in Sonnenfinsternis gesät

so fallen wir
so fallen wir.

Thus it is said

Thus it is said—
set down in serpentine lines

Fall.

The sun
chinese mandala
holy twisted ornament
returned home into inner phases
fixed smile
prayed away
dragon of light
belching fire against time
shield-bearer was the fallen fruit of earth
once
gleaming with gold—

Pointing at prophecies
with fingers of flame:

This is the star
peeled to the point of death—

This is the apple's core
sown in the sun's eclipse

thus we fall
thus we fall.

Vertriebene

Vertriebene
aus Wohnungen
Windgepeitschte
mit der Sterbeader hinter dem Ohr
die Sonne erschlagend—

Aus verlorenen Sitten geworfen
dem Gang der Gewässer folgend
dem weinenden Geländer des Todes
halten oft noch in der Höhle
des Mundes
ein Wort versteckt
aus Angst vor Dieben

sagen: Rosmarin
und kauen eine Wurzel
aus dem Acker gezogen
oder
schmecken nächtelang: Abschied
sagen:
Die Zeit ist um
wenn eine neue Wunde aufbrach
im Fuss.

Reissend wird ihr Leib
im Salz der Marter fortgefressen.

Hautlos
augenlos
hat Hiob Gott gebildet.

Those expelled

Those expelled
from dwellings
whipped by the wind
with the vein of death behind the ear
slaying the sun—

Cast out of lost customs
following the course of the waters
the weeping railings of death
often still hide a word
in the hollow of the mouth
for fear of thieves

saying: rosemary
and chewing a root
pulled from the field
or
tasting for many nights: farewell
saying:
The time is gone
when a new wound opened
in the foot.

Their bodies are ravenously
eaten away in the salt of torment.

Skinless
eyeless
Job created God.

Kleiner Frieden

Kleiner Frieden
in der durchsichtigen Stunde
am Levkojengrab
im Abendrot trompetet Jenseits.

Gloriole des Palmenblattes
Wüstenoffenbarung der Einsamkeit.

Der Ahne Leben
im leuchtenden Andachtsbuch
ruhend auf Murmelbaches Schlummerrolle
und Muschel an das Ohr gelegt
mit Spieluhrmelodie.

O grosser Ozean im kleinen Ohr!
O Menuett der Liebe
oblatenzartes Stundenbuch

auch das war Leben—
der gleiche Schlaf in schwarz Magie
und Dorn der die vergessene Rose
des Blutes
in Erinnerung sticht

gezähnter Blitz
in des Gewitters Maskentanz
verdunkelnd
auch diese Elfenbeinküste.

Small peace

Small peace
in the transparent hour
at the gillyflower grave
the beyond trumpets in the sunset.

Gloriole of the palm leaf
desert-revelation of loneliness.

The ancestor's life
in the glowing book of devotion
resting on the bolster of the murmuring brook
and shell laid to the ear
with musical-box melody.

O great ocean in the little ear!
O minuet of love
wafer-thin book of hours

that too was life—
the same sleep in black magic
and thorn which in memory
pricks the forgotten
rose of blood

jagged lightning
in the masked dance of storm
darkening
also this ivory coast.

Hier ist kein Bleiben länger

Hier ist kein Bleiben länger
denn aus seinem Grunde spricht schon Meer
die Brust der Nacht
hebt atmend hoch
die Wand, daran ein Kopf
mit schwerer Traumgeburt gelehnt.

In diesem Baustoff
war kein Sternenfinger
mit im Spiel
seit das Gemisch im Sand begann
so lebend noch im Tod.

Wer weint
der sucht nach seiner Melodie
die hat der Wind
musikbelaubt
in Nacht versteckt.

Frisch von der Quelle
ist zu weit entfernt.

Zeit ists zu fliegen
nur mit unserem Leib.

Here is no further stay

Here is no further stay
for the sea is already speaking from its depth
the breast of night
breathing
lifts the wall, on which a head
leans with heavy dream-birth.

No star-finger
was involved
in this building material
since the mixture in the sand began
thus living even in death.

Whoever weeps
seeks his melody
which the wind
leafy with music
has hidden in night.

Fresh from the source
is too far away.

It is time to fly
but with our bodies.

Mutter

Mutter
Meerzeitgeblüh
nächtlicher Ort
für der Ozeane Arom
und die Niederkunft
des erleuchteten Sandes—

Umzogen von göttlicher Ellipse
mit den beiden Schwellenbränden
Eingang
und
Ausgang.

Dein Atemzug holt Zeiten heim
Bausteine für Herzkammern
und das himmlische Echo der Augen.

Der Mond hat sein Schicksal
in deine Erwartung gesenkt.

Leise vollendet sich
die schlafende Sprache
von Wasser und Wind

im Raum deines
lerchenhaften Aufschreis.

Mother

Mother
flower of ocean's time
nocturnal place
for scent of the sea
and the childbirth
of the illuminated sand—

Surrounded by divine ellipse
with the two threshold fires
entrance
and exit.

Your breath brings ages home
building-stones for the chambers of the heart
and the heavenly echo of the eyes.

The moon has sunk its fate
into your expectation.

Softly the sleeping speech
of water and wind
consummates itself

in the space
of your lark-like outcry.

Lange

Lange
sichelte Jakob
mit seines Armes Segen
die Ähren der Jahrtausende
die in Todesschlaf hängenden
nieder—
sah
mit Blindenaugen—
hielt Sonnen und Sterne
einen Lichtblick umarmt—
bis es endlich hüpfte
wie Geburt aus seiner Hand
und
in Rembrandts Augenhimmel hinein.

Joseph
schnell noch
versuchte den Blitz
des falschen Segens
abzuleiten
der aber brannte schon
Gott-wo-anders auf—

Und der Erstgeborene losch
wie Asche—

For a long time

For a long time
Jacob
raising his arm in blessing
reaped with a sickle
the wheat ears of the millennia
which hung down in the sleep
of death—
saw
with blind eyes—
held suns and stars
embraced in a look of light—
until at last something hopped
like birth from his hand
and
into the sky of Rembrandt's eye.

Joseph
quickly
tried to divert
the lightning
of the false blessing
but it was already leaping up
God knows where—

And the firstborn extinct
like ashes—

Halleluja

Selbst die Steine umarmen wir—
wir haben einen Pakt mit ihnen geschlossen—
HIOB

Halleluja
bei der Geburt eines Felsens—

Milde Stimme aus Meer
fliessende Arme
auf und ab
halten Himmel und Grab—

Und dann:
Fanfare
in der Corona des Salzes
ozeangeliebtes
wanderndes Zeitalter
stösst granitgehörnt
in seinen Morgen—

Halleluja
im Quarz und Glimmerstein

beflügelte Sehnsucht
hat ihren Schlüssel himmelwärts gedreht
Tief-Nacht-Geburt
aber schon Heimat für eines Seevogels
Ruhesturz

Feuerflüchtlinge
aus blinden Verstecken entflohen
ausgewinterte Chemie
in geheimer Unterhaltung des Aufbruchs—

Hallelujah

We even embrace the stars—
we have made a pact with them—
                    JOB

Hallelujah
at the birth of a rock—

Soft voice of sea
arms flowing
up and down
hold sky and grave—

And then:
fanfare
in the corona of salt
ocean-loved
wandering age
thrusts granite-horned
into its morning—

Hallelujah
in quartz and mica

winged longing
has turned its key heavenwards
deep-night-birth
but home already for a sea-bird's
plunging repose

fire-fugitives
fled from blind hiding places
chemistry dead with cold
in secret conversation of decampment—

Sonnensamen
aus geöffneten Mündern der Offenbarung

Halleluja
der Steine im Licht—

Versiegelte Sterngewänder
durchbrochen
und der Himmel mit der ziehenden Sprache
öffnet Augen an umweinter Nacktheit—

Aber
im Mutterwasser
saugende Algen umklammern
den füssehebenden Dunkelleib
Fische in Hochzeitskammern
wo Sintflut bettet
reigen besessen
gefolterte Träume gerinnen
in der Meduse atmend Saphirgeblüh
und wie mit Wegweisern zeigend
Blutkorallen aus schläfrigem Tod—

Halleluja
bei der Geburt eines Felsens

in die goldene Weide des Lichts—

sun-seed
from open mouths of revelation

Hallelujah
of the stones in light—

Sealed gowns of stars
openwork
and the sky with the dragging language
opens eyes at wept-for nakedness—

But
in the maternal water
sucking algae cling to
the foot-lifting body of darkness
fish in bridal chambers
where deluge beds
dancing possessed
tortured dreams congeal
in the Medusa's breathing sapphire-blossom
and pointing as with signposts
blood-coral from sleepy death—

Hallelujah
at the birth of a rock

into the golden meadow of light—

Schlaf webt das Atemnetz

Schlaf webt das Atemnetz
heilige Schrift
aber niemand ist hier lesekundig
ausser den Liebenden
die flüchten hinaus
durch die singend kreisenden
Kerker der Nächte
traumgebunden die Gebirge
der Toten
übersteigend

um dann nur noch
in Geburt zu baden
ihrer eigenen
hervorgetöpferten Sonne—

Sleep weaves the net of breath

Sleep weaves the net of breath
holy scripture
but no one here can read
except lovers
who flee out
through the singing circling
dungeons of the nights
surmounting
dreambound
the mountains of the dead

only then
to bathe in the birth
of their own
hand-turned sun—

Es springt

Es springt
dieses Jahrhundert
aus seinem abgeschuppten Todkalender—

Es pfeift um das Haar der Berenice
ein Peitschenblitz—

Es hat sich Adams Haupt geöffnet
empor steigt zuckend
in den dünnen Strich der Luft:

Die sieben Tage Schöpfung.

Es spriesst ein Samenkorn in Angst
schnell auf einem Menschenfinger.
Der Adler trägt im Schnabel seinen Kinderhorst.

Einen Kuss gab noch der Bienensaug der Mädchenlippe
dann sichelt der Tod das Windgetreide.

Entgleiste Sterne werden nachtschwarz angestrichen
erlöst sprühen die fünf Sinne wie Leuchtraketen auf—

Und Schweigen ist ein neues Land—

This century

This century
springs
from its descaled calendar of death—

A whipped lightning
whistles round Berenice's hair—

Adam's head has opened
climbs trembling
into the thin strip of air:

The seven days of creation.

A seed sprouts quickly in fear
on a human finger.
The eagle bears its children's eyrie in its beak.

The bee-suck kissed the maiden lip once more
then death reaped the wheat of the wind.

Stars fallen from their orbits are being painted black
redeemed the five senses blaze like Very lights—

And silence is a new land—

Ohne Kompass

Ohne Kompass
Taumelkelch im Meer
und
die Windrose des Blutes tanzend
im Streit mit allen Himmelslichtern
so der Jüngling—

Versucht seine Jugend
mit dem Gegenwind im Haar
weiss noch nichts von der Vorsicht
des Schattens in blendender Sonne.

Auf seinem Lärmgott
durchschneidet er
des sinkenden Abends flehende Hände
und pfeift die Bettelei des Alters
in den Wind.

Die Nacht
entgürtet er der Sterne
wirft
diese abgedufteten Lavendellieder
der Urmutter
zwischen die Leinewand.

Doch steigt er gerne die Treppe
zum Himmel hinauf
die Aussicht zu erweitern
denn er ist gespannt von Tod
wie ein Blitz
ohne Wiederkehr.

Without compass

Without compass
reeling chalice in the sea
the compass card of blood dancing
in strife with all the lights of heaven
thus the young man—

Tests his youth
with the headwind in his hair
knows nothing yet of the shadow's
caution in the blinding sun.

On his noisy god
he cuts through
the suppliant hands of sinking evening
and whistles the beggary of age
into the wind.

He ungirdles
the stars from night
casts
these scentless lavender-songs
of the mother of mankind
between the linen sheets.

But he gladly climbs the stair
to heaven
to broaden the view
for he is tense with death
like lightning
without return.

Von den Schaukelstühlen
heimisch gewordener Geschlechter
stösst er sich ab

ausser sich geraten
mit dem Feuerhelm
verwundet er die Nacht.

Aber
einmal fällt Stille ein
diese Insel
gelagert schon
an letzter Atemspitze des Lebens
und
aus zeitverfallendem Stern
tönt Musik
nicht fürs Ohr—

Er aber
hört das Samenkorn flüstern

im Tod—

He thrusts himself off
from the rocking chairs
of domesticated generations

beside himself
with the fire helmet
he wounds the night.

But
one day silence will fall
this island
already placed
at the last breathing point of life
and
from a time-expiring star
music will sound
not for the ear—

But he
will hear the seed whispering

in death—

Weit fort

Weit fort
von den Kirchhöfen
weine ich um dich
aber auch nicht in die Lüfte
und nicht in das wartende Meer.

Weit fort
von allen längst verschmerzten
Zeitaltern
in Mumiensteinen
eingesargten—

Nur in die Sehnsucht
das wachsende Element
lege ich meine Träne—

Hier ist ausserhalb und innen.

Diese Lichterpyramide
ausgemessen in anderen Räumen
mit Begrabenen von allen Königreichen
bis ans Ende der Trauer—

Mit den Altären der Seele
die ihr Sakrament
lange schon hinter dem Augenlid
verbargen—

Far away

Far away
from the churchyards
I weep for you
but not into the air
nor into the waiting sea.

Far away
from all long since endured
ages
coffined
in mummy stones—

Only into longing
the growing element
I lay my tear—

Here is without and within.

This pyramid of light
measured out in other rooms
with the buried of all kingdoms
until the end of sorrow—

With the altars of the soul
which long ago
hid their sacrament
behind the eyelid—

Wo nur sollen wir hinter den Nebeln

Wo nur sollen wir hinter den Nebeln
die Wurzel der Hauche suchen
die in den Wolken Augenblicks-Schöpfungsgeschichte
    schreiben?
Was zieht da ein in den windigen Leib
für mutterloses Gesicht?
Welche Ader zersprang um der heiligen Geometrie der
    Sehnsucht
in deinen Augen Heimat zu geben?

Mit Wasserblumen
weinend ausgeziert
fliegt die Waise im hellgrünen Gras
erfundene Umarmung
lange vor des Menschen Eintritt
in den Lehm.

Das Neue ist Gottes—
Seine Erstlinge dort oben winken
Verwandtschaft.
Eva umschlängelt
spielt Erdapfelspiel.

Einmal beschworen
der Stier stösst gesichelt durch Zeiten
sein Bild gewebt in hautloser Glorie—

Geistesgestört flattert Prophetenbart
abgerissen von der Botschaft der Lippe
Moment des wandernden Schrittes
und der Gebärde des Tragens
ehe sie in die Schwergewichte der Menschengeburt fielen
im Schrei—

306

But where behind the mists shall we

But where behind the mists shall we
seek the roots of the breaths
which write in the clouds the creation myth of the moment?
What kind of motherless face
enters the airy body?
Which vein burst in order to give the holy geometry of
        longing
a homeland in your eyes?

The orphan flies in the light green grass
adorned with weeping
water-flowers
an invented embrace
long before man's entry
into the clay.

What is new is God's—
His firstborn there above signal
kinship.
Eve ensnaked
plays the apple-of-earth game.

Once evoked
the bull thrust sickled through ages
his image woven in skinless glory—

Prophet's beard flutters madly
torn off from the lips' message
moment of the wandering step
and the gesture of being burdened
before they fell shrieking into the laborious gravities
of human birth—

Welche Finsternisse

Welche Finsternisse
hinterm Augenlid
angeglänzt
von der explodierenden Abendsonne
des Heimwehs

Strandgut
mit dem Seezeichen
königlich
schlafbewachsen

Schiffbruch
Hände aus den Wellen
fliehende Versuche
Gott zu fangen

Bussweg
umarmend
Meilensteine aus Meer

O keine Ankunft
ohne Tod—

What darknesses

What darknesses
behind the eyelid
lit by
the exploding evening sun
of homesickness

Jetsam
with the sea mark
royally
sleep-encrusted

Shipwreck
hands from the waves
fleeting attempts
to trap God

Path of penitence
embracing
milestone of sea

Oh, no arrival
without death—

Wenn der Atem

Wenn der Atem
die Hütte der Nacht errichtet hat
und ausgeht
seinen wehenden Himmelsort zu suchen

und der Leib
der blutende Weinberg
die Fässer der Stille angefüllt hat
die Augen übergegangen sind
in das sehende Licht

wenn ein jedes sich in sein Geheimnis
verflüchtigte
und alles doppelt getan ist—
Geburt
alle Jakobsleitern der Todesorgeln hinaufsingt

dann
zündet ein schönes Wettergeleucht
die Zeit an—

When breath

When breath
has erected the hut of night
and goes out
to seek its drifting place in the sky

and the body
the bleeding vineyard
has filled the casks of silence
and the eyes have merged
into the visionary light

when each has melted
into his mystery
and all is doubly done—
birth
will sing up all Jacob's ladders of death's organs

then
a lovely sheet-lightning
will ignite time—

Ende

Ende
aber nur in einem Zimmer—
denn
über die Schulter mir schaut
nicht dein Gesicht
aber
wohnhaft in Luft
und Nichts
Maske aus Jenseits

und Anruf
Hof nur aus Segen herum
und nicht zu nah
an brennbarer Wirklichkeit

und Anruf wieder
und ich gefaltet eng und kriechend
in Verpuppung zurück
ohne Flügelzucken
und werde fein gesiebt
eine Braut
in den durstenden Sand—

End

End
but only in one room—
for it is not your face
which looks over my shoulder
but
dwelling in air
and nothingness
a mask from beyond

and summons
encircled by halo made only of blessing
and not too close
to flammable reality

and again summons
and I tightly folded and creeping
back into the chrysalis
with no twitch of wings
am being finely sieved
a bride
into the thirsting sand—

Tod

Tod
Meergesang
spülend um meinen Leib
salzige Traube
durstlockende in meinem Mund—

Aufschlägst du die Saiten meiner Adern
bis sie singend springen
knospend aus den Wunden
die Musik meiner Liebe zu spielen—

Deine entfächerten Horizonte
mit der Zackenkrone aus Sterben
schon um den Hals gelegt
das Ritual des Aufbruchs
mit dem gurgelnden Laut der Atemzüge
begonnen
verliessest du nach Verführerart
vor der Hochzeit das bezauberte Opfer
entkleidet schon fast bis auf den Sand
verstossen
aus zwei Königreichen
nur noch Seufzer
zwischen Nacht und Nacht—

Death

Death
song of the sea
washing around my body
salty grape
thirst-tempting in my mouth—

You pluck the strings of my veins
until they leap singing
budding from the wounds
to play the music of my love—

Your fan-spread horizons
with the scalloped crown of dying
already laid round the neck
the ritual of departure
begun
with the gurgling sound of breathing
you left as a seducer leaves
the enchanted victim before the wedding
unclothed almost down to the sand
cast out
of two kingdoms
only sighs still
between night and night—

Inmitten

Inmitten
der Leidensstation
besessen von einem Lächeln
gibst du Antwort
denen
die im Schatten fragen
mit dem Mund voll gottverzogener Worte
aufgehämmert
aus der Vorzeit der Schmerzen.

Die Liebe hat kein Sterbehemd mehr an
versponnen der Raum
im Faden deiner Sehnsucht.
Gestirne prallen rückwärts ab
von deinen Augen
diesem
leise verkohlenden Sonnenstoff

aber über deinem Haupte
der Meeresstern der Gewissheit
mit den Pfeilen der Auferstehung
leuchtet rubinrot—

Obsessed by a smile

Obsessed by a smile
at the station
of the cross
you answer
those
who ask in the shadow
with your mouth full of God-distorted words
hammered-on
from the foretime of pain.

Love no longer wears a shroud
the room entangles
in the thread of your longing.
Constellations rebound
from your eyes
of
gently carbonizing solar matter

but above your head
certainty's star of the sea
with the arrows of resurrection
glowing ruby-red—

Ach dass man so wenig begreift
solange die Augen nur Abend wissen.
Fenster und Türen öffnen sich wie entgleist
vor dem Aufbruchbereiten..

Unruhe flammt
Verstecke für Falter
die Heimat zu beten beginnen.

Bis endlich dein Herz
die schreckliche Angelwunde
in ihre Heilung gerissen wurde
Himmel und Erde
als Asche sich küssten in deinem Blick—

O Seele—verzeih
dass ich zurück dich führen gewollt
an so viele Herde der Ruhe

Ruhe
die doch nur ein totes Oasenwort ist—

Oh, that one understands so little
as long as the eyes know only evening.
Windows and doors open as if derailed
before the preparation for departure.

Unrest flames
hiding places for butterflies
which begin to pray "home."

Until at last your heart
the terrible wound of the hook
was torn into healing
heaven and earth
kissed as ashes in your glance—

O soul—forgive me
that I wanted to lead you back
to so many hearths of rest

Rest
which is only a dead oasis-word—

Alle landmessenden Finger

Alle landmessenden Finger
erheben sich
von den Staubgrenzen
und
augenbesät
das Tuch der Cherubim um die Schläfen
so sieht der Blick
durch entleerte Linse der Sonne.

Schlaf überfällt Dächer und Wände.

Auch der Engel hat Abschied genommen
bekränzt mit Traum.

Rauschend am Gehör vorbei
das Floss
beseelt mit dir

Wir sind
nur wir

All land-surveying fingers

All land-surveying fingers
rise
from the borders of dust
and
sown with eyes
the cloth of the cherubim around the temples
thus the glance sees
through the emptied lens of the sun.

Sleep conquers roofs and walls.

The angel has also said farewell
wreathed in dream.

Roaring past my ears
the raft
inspired by you

We are
only we

Angeängstigt

Angeängstigt
mit dem Einhorn Schmerz durchstochen—

Wächter
Wächter
ist die Nacht schon um?

O du Drama schwarze Zeit
mit unendlichem Gerede
hinter dornverschlossenem Mund.

Blitze
salzversteinert wetzen
Reue die im Blut begraben—

Wächter
Wächter
sage deinem Herrn:
Es ist durchlitten—

und
Zeit den Scheiterhaufen
anzuzünden
der Morgen singt
und nachtgeronnen Blut
im Hahnenschrei
soll fliessen—

Made fearful

Made fearful
pierced with the unicorn pain—

Watchman
watchman
is the night over yet?

O you tragedy black time
with unending talk
behind the thorn-sealed mouth.

Lightnings
salt-petrified sharpen
penitence buried in the blood—

Watchman
watchman
tell your master:
Suffering is over—

and
time to light
the pyre
the morning sings
and night-congealed blood
shall flow
in the cockcrow—

Eine Garbe Blitze

Eine Garbe Blitze
fremde Macht
besetzen
diesen Acker aus Papier
Worte lodern
tödliches Begreifen
Donner schlägt das Haus ein
darin Grablegung geschah.

Nach Vergebung dieses Lebens
aus verzehrter Schreibeweise
aus der einzigsten Sekunde
hebt der innere Ozean
seine weisse Schweigekrone
in die Seligkeit zu dir—

A sheaf of lightning

A sheaf of lightning
alien power
occupies
this field of paper
words flame
deathly comprehension
thunder strikes down the house
in which burial took place.

After this life's forgiveness
out of ravaged styles of writing
out of the only second
the inner ocean lifts
its white crown of silence
to you in eternal bliss—

So rann ich aus dem Wort

So rann ich aus dem Wort:

Ein Stück der Nacht
mit Armen ausgebreitet
nur eine Waage
Fluchten abzuwiegen
diese Sternenzeit
versenkt in Staub
mit den gesetzten Spuren.

Jetzt ist es spät.
Das Leichte geht aus mir
und auch das Schwere
die Schultern fahren schon
wie Wolken fort
Arme und Hände
ohne Traggebärde.

Tiefdunkel ist des Heimwehs Farbe immer

so nimmt die Nacht
mich wieder in Besitz.

Thus I ran out of the word

Thus I ran out of the word:

A piece of night
with arms outspread
only a scale
to weigh flights
this star-time
sunk into dust
with the fixed tracks.

Now it is late.
The lightness leaves me
and the heaviness as well
my shoulders already
sail away like clouds
arms and hands
without gesture of burden.

The color of homecoming is always deep and dark

thus the night
possesses me again.

Journey into a Dustless Realm

Translated by Ruth and Matthew Mead

Auf dem Markt

Auf dem Markt
Sonnengenährtes schläft
hingerichtete Natur—
bald wird in deinen Mund
die Tomate explodieren

Aber plötzlich
zahlend die Währung
ein Wallgraben aus Nacht
umringt alles Tun
keine Zugbrücke aufgezogen
zum Händler
der seine Hand ausstreckt
um einzunehmen

Die abgeschnittene Schöpfung
auf den Ladentischen
wurde in meine Welt verlegt
um das Gebet zu finden
das die verstümmelten Silben zusammenfügt
in ihre dunkle Harmonie
darin die Ideogramme sich küssen und heilen.

In the market

In the market
what the sun nourishes sleeps
executed nature—
soon the tomato
will explode in your mouth

But suddenly
paying the money
a moat of night
surrounds all action
no drawbridge drawn up
to the dealer
who stretches out his hand
to take

The cut-off creation
on the shop counter
was placed into my world
to find the prayer
which joins the mutilated syllables
into their dark harmony
in which the ideograms kiss and heal.

Der Umriss

Dies ist übrig—
mit meiner Welt zogst du hinaus
Komet des Todes.
Übrig ist die Umarmung
der Leere
ein kreisender Ring
der seinen Finger verlor.

Wieder Schwärze
vor der Schöpfung
Trauergesetz.
Abgeblättert die leichtsinnige Vergoldung
der Nacht
die sich der Tag erlaubte.

Der Schatten Kalligraphie
als Nachlass.

Grüngefärbte Landschaften
mit ihren wahrsagenden Gewässern
ertrunken
in den Sackgassen der Finsternis.

Bett Stuhl und Tisch
schlichen auf Zehenspitzen aus dem Zimmer
dem Haar der Trennung nach—

Alles ist ausgewandert mit dir
mein ganzer Besitz enteignet—

nur trinkst du Geliebtestes mir
die Worte vom Atem
bis ich verstumme—

The Outline

This remains—
with my world you went away
Comet of death.
The embrace
of the void remains
a circling ring
which has lost its finger.

Again darkness
before the creation
law of mourning.
Peeled off the frivolous gilding
of the night
which the day permitted itself.

The shadow calligraphy
as legacy.

Green-colored landscapes
with their prophetic waters
drowned
in the cul-de-sacs of darkness.

Bed chair and table
stole on tiptoe from the room
following the hair of parting—

Everything has gone with you
all I possessed expropriated—

only you my beloved
drink the words from my breath
until I grow silent—

Death Still Celebrates Life

Translated by Ruth and Matthew Mead

Eine Schöpfungsminute im Auge des Baalschem

Mitten im Jahrhundert—das Jahr steigt,
ein Flüchtling, in die Luft—Renner ohne Scheuklappen
schleppend die Kette seiner Tage, alle angezündet von
      Besessenheit
und mit Feuerhänden betend dorthin wo
der Landvermesser Krieg noch Platz gelassen
für die Halluzination einer Grenzübersteigung.

Denn auf dem Himalaja der Qualen
bluten auf grünen Kindertraumwiesen
gemeinsam Sieger und Besiegte damit
künftige Morgen und Abende ihre Farbe
nicht vergessen in der grossen Sterbeschlacht.

Wenn auch die alte Frau im Herdrauch blinzelt
und im kräutersegnenden Mond Kaffee beschwört
aus verstorbenen Eichelhülsen—
Und der Berg seine Höhle auftut
für den Heiligen, der seinen Mantel schürzen muss
und einige Sterne an den Hut stecken
im Dunkeln—ehe er die Gebete der Verfolgten
die vom Fussboden bis zum Himmel aufgebahrt sind
mit Heimweh beflügeln kann—

Und das Jahr in Wehen gekrümmt und in
lange schon ausgerechneter Geometrie
rauchend am Schwanz des Kometen
mit abgehäuteten Tagen hängend
fast schon nicht mehr wahr im Massengrab des Schlafes.

A Minute of Creation in Baalshem's Eye

Mid-century—the year climbs,
a fugitive, into the air—runner without blinkers
dragging the chain of its days, all afire with obsession
and praying with hands of fire to where
war the surveyor of land has still left room
for the hallucination of a frontier crossing.

For on the Himalayas of torment
victor and vanquished bleed together
in green meadows of children's dreams
so that future mornings and evenings do not forget
their colors in the great battle of death.

Even though the old woman blinks in the smoke of the hearth
and conjures coffee from dead acorn-shells
by herb-blessing moonlight—
And the hill opens its cave
for the saint who has to tuck up his coat
and stick several stars in his hat
in darkness—before he can wing with homesickness
the prayers of the persecuted which are piled up
from floor to sky—

And the year bent double in labor and in
long-since-calculated geometry
smoking at the comet's tail
hanging with skinned days
almost no longer true in the mass grave of sleep.

337

Alles Herzklopfen der Versteckten drängt zum Wirt
der mit seinen hohen Bauernstiefeln oben schnell
am Himmel schreitet oder
unten einen Gast bedient.

Alles sucht Asyl bei ihm, der sich auftut—wächst und weitet
nach der Richtung Ewigkeit.

Und es ist Nacht, die sich geladen hat
mit Sprengstoff des Erwachens, und aufspringt
das Geheimnis der Sekunde—entstirnte schon
in Baalschems ungebrochenem Blick, der zieht
am Faden der Gnade Leben und Tod
in Gottversöhnung hoch.

Und die Farbe *Nichts* lugt nachtentfärbend
aus dem Opfertod der Zeiten
wenn der Heilige tanzend die Gebete weitersagt
die sie im Geäst der Adern hängen liessen
oder zur Entzündung einer Martersonne.

Allen die nur bis zur Grenze glauben
wo Gestirne noch die Uhren stellen
schenkt er die Sekunde, die sein Augen-Blick
für das Unsichtbare vorbereitet—
im Geburtenbett der Tränen aufgefangen hat.

Every heartbeat of those in hiding pulses to the landlord
who strides swiftly in his high farming boots
above in the sky or
serves a guest below.

Everything seeks refuge in him, he opens—grows and broadens
in the direction of eternity.

And it is night, which is self-charged
with dynamite of awakening and explodes
the secret of the second—already without stars
in Baalshem's unbroken stare which draws
life and death on the thread of grace
high into God's reconciliation.

And the color *Nothing* peeps, draining night of color,
from the expiatory death of ages
when the saint dancing repeats the prayers
which they left hanging in the branches of the veins
or for the lighting of a sun of torment.

To all whose belief reaches only to the border
where constellations still set the clocks
he gives the second which his glance,
prepared for the invisible—
has caught in the natal bed of tears.

Sehr leise im Kreislauf gleitet

Sehr leise im Kreislauf gleitet
die vom Saturn mit Melancholie Gekrönte
durch Milchstrassen der Fremdheit
wenn im Mund der übers Kreuz Gesegneten
die Buchstaben in kriegerischer Strategie
einander umbringen—

da hängt sie zwischen vergitterten Kranken
an einem Goldhaar des Sonnensystems
das weinende Lächeln im Schlafsaal der Nacht.

She crowned with melancholy by Saturn

She crowned with melancholy by Saturn
glides very softly in orbit
through alien Milky Ways
when in the mouth of those blessed above the cross
the letters kill each other
in warlike strategy—

there she hangs between the imprisoned sick
on a gold hair of the solar system
the weeping smile in the dormitory of night.

Auf der äussersten Spitze der Landzunge
Ausgangsverbot
Abgrund droht süchtiger Schwerkraft
Franziskus—Baalschem übersteigen heiliges Fasten
glänzen im Nichts—
Der Ölberg betet mit dem einzigen Schrei
der dem Stein ein Herz zerriss
Musik der Agonie
ins Ohr des Universums
das mit Welten Stigmatisierte
entzündet seine Umgangssprache—

On the utmost tip of the spit of land

On the utmost tip of the spit of land
curfew
abyss threatens addicted gravity
St. Francis—Baalshem, overstep the holy fast
shining in nothing—
The Mount of Olives prays with the single cry
which tore the stone's heart
music of agony
in the ear of the universe
that which is stigmatized by worlds
ignites its own colloquial language—

343

Niemand unter den Zuschauenden

Niemand unter den Zuschauenden
will sich die Fusspitzen netzen denn die
welche Land verlassen mit einem Sprung
vergessen Amen zu sagen nach ihrem Gebet
weil dort wo die Weberin ihre Schiffe aussetzt
und in die Nacht schickt
Oceana ihre Überschwemmungen beginnt
und die Goldader der Sterblichen
unter Wasserbewusstsein sinkt
und arbeitet in der Tiefe für Gott.

Wohl lauscht auch der Arzt am Herzen Ertrinkender
wie an dem abgewanderten Gesang einer Muschel
die über den Königsweg der Geheimnisse schwebt
dort—wo die Erstlinge der Landlosen wohnen—

No one among the onlookers

No one among the onlookers
wants to wet his toes for they
who leave land with a leap
forget to end their prayer with an Amen
for there where the weaver launches her shuttles
sending them into the night
Oceana begins her floodings
and the gold vein of mortals
sinks below the water level of consciousness
and labors for God in the depth.

Well may the physician listen at the hearts of the drowned
as at the seashell's retreating song
which sways across the royal road of mystery
there—where the firstborn of the landless dwell—

Im eingefrorenen Zeitalter der Anden

Im eingefrorenen Zeitalter der Anden
die Prinzessin im Eissarg
umarmt von kosmischer Liebe
Auferstehungsklar
mit dem Schicksal der Toten beschrieben schon
dem wurzelsuchenden gebückten Blick
Nachtgeschau—
unbehelligt von Auflösungssucht der Elemente
bis an die dunkle Kraft des Vaters—

da—hier—
steht sie—
Ferne im Fleisch gefangen
Zeichen für Untiefen
stumm leuchtend
blind atmendes Meergewächs—

Inmitten der rauchenden Arche der Angstträume
aller flüchtenden Vergangenheitsschlepper
steht sie—
eine Gesalbte schon—

Inmitten der aus zanksüchtigen Sprachen neu errichteten
babylonischen Türme
und Pyramiden sehnsuchtsverrenkt
für häusliches Sterben vermessen
steht sie

während die immer rinnende Endzeit im Ohr
die Rede der Ausgesetzten führt—

In the frozen age of the Andes

In the frozen age of the Andes
the princess in the coffin of ice
embraced by cosmic love
resurrection-clear
with the fate of the dead already described
to the bent root-seeking glance
night-vision—
unencumbered by the elements' urge to dissolve
unto the father's dark power—

there—here—
she stands—
distance caught in the flesh
sign for shallows
silently shining
blindly breathing ocean-growth—

Amid the smoking ark of the nightmares
of all fugitives who drag their past behind them
she stands—
already anointed—

Amid the new towers of Babylon built
of quarrelsome languages
and pyramids twisted by longing
measured out for domestic dying
she stands

while in her ear the ever-flowing end of time
speaks for the outcasts—

Wortlos spielt sie mit einem Aquamarin

Wortlos spielt sie mit einem Aquamarin
aus dem Treugelöbnis ihrer Vorzeit—
dieser blaue Himmel ist von einem Kuss ihres Geliebten
      bewohnt
mit einer Omega-Umarmung gibt sie ihm Ort—Dasein—und
      Grabstätte.
Ihr Adernetz umfasst die Liebe
ihr Leben ist gerettet.
Wortlos liebt sie die Tonleiter entlang—
sie ist die Sanftmut im irrlichternden Haus
Verlassenwerden heisst für sie
für Zwei nun weiterlieben
von Treulosigkeit ins Himmelreich zu springen—

Nicht geht sie auf Wanderschaft
mit ihrem rieselnden Staub
sie isst die süsse Sonntagsspeise
und küsst den Stein
und horcht auf seine blaue Sprache
der Lichterjahre im Millionenfunkeln

Aber Meere sind schon aufgelöste Liebende
im leisen Seligwerden ihres Blutes—

Wordlessly she plays with an aquamarine

Wordlessly she plays with an aquamarine
from her betrothal long ago—
a kiss of her beloved dwells in this blue sky
with an omega-embrace she gives him place—being—and
        tomb.
The net of her veins encloses love
her life is saved.
Wordlessly she loves along the scale—
she is the meekness in the jack-o'-lantern house
being alone now means for her
to go on loving for two
to leap from unfaithfulness into heaven—

She never takes the road
with her trickling dust
she eats dessert on Sunday
and kisses the stone
and listens to its blue speech
of lightyears in millions of sparks

But dissolved lovers are already oceans
in the soft bliss of her blood—

Anders gelegt die Adern

Anders gelegt die Adern
schon in der Frühe des Mutterleibes
rückwärts buchstabiert deines Lichtes Geknospe
dann—in der Welt der Symbole mit grossem Umweg
zurück in den Sand—
und mit Hämmern dein Herzschlag
auf die Schatten der Zeit
diese zerfetzten Glieder der Nächte—

Von den grünen Wiesen der Kindheit
unterm grabesduftenden Buchsbaum
rufst du heim
ein neues Alphabet in den Worten
Baumeister du und Gründer von Städten und Pflanzungen
von blutenden Weinbergen in den Malereien der Lüfte
eingezaubert in die Alchemie deines Auges—

Schwester—Schwester
mit dem Kartenspiel der Gesichte und
dem Ebenholzschrecken
und von der Flammentracht der Schergen belagert—
gegen Untergang senken sich deine Gebete
wenn die Koralle des Morgens verwaist—

Laid differently the veins

Laid differently the veins
in the morning of the womb
spelled backwards the budding of your light
then—in the world of symbols with a great detour
back into the sand—
and with hammers your heartbeat
on the shadows of time
these torn limbs of nights—

From the green meadows of childhood
under the box-tree smelling of the grave
you call home
a new alphabet in the words
you builder and founder of cities and fields
of bleeding vineyards in the paintings of the air
conjured into the alchemy of your eye—

Sister—sister
with the card pack of faces and
the ebony horror
and besieged by the executioners' garb of flame—
as downfall nears your prayers sink
when the coral of morning is deserted—

Rückgängig gemacht ist die Verlobung
der Heimgesuchten

Rückgängig gemacht ist die Verlobung der Heimgesuchten
im Weltenraum
das Meer steigt auf am vorderen Gesicht
und teilt sich nicht—
Der Wind reisst zurück die Wurzelsuchenden—
Der Nacht wurde ein kristallen Kabinett
der Spiegelfechterei eingebaut
darin die Bilder auf schiefen Ebenen heruntergleissen—
Rettung nur mit Himmelskunde möglich
wenn die magischen Einschiffungen
am Flügel der Cherubim aus den verwilderten Augenge-
    wässern gezogen werden—

The betrothal of the afflicted is annulled

The betrothal of the afflicted is annulled
in space
the sea rises at the foremost face
and does not divide—
The wind tears back those who seek roots—
Into the night was built a crystal room
of make-believe
in which the images glitter down uneven levels—
Rescue only possible with knowledge of astronomy
when the magical embarkations
are drawn from the wild water of the eye by cherubim wings—

Im Park Spazierengehen

Im Park Spazierengehen—
vorbei an den Wegweisern, die Sternbilder der Unruhe
mit Nummern bezeichnen
wo in den Krankensälen das Sterben liegen blieb
vielleicht schon in die Hierarchie der hohen Werke
        eingegangen—

nun im Freien—
die Glieder schon ausser sich
das neue Zeitalter der lippenlosen Sprache des Wachstums
zu ergreifen
die rauschende—duftende—malende—

Der Fuss in der Traumkunst des Schwebens unterwiesen
von der sprengenden Kraft des Dunkels.

Davids Tanz
vor dem Mirakel
die knospenden Welten in der Bundeslade führend—

Im Park Spazierengehen—
die Eingeweihten
nur vom Stimmband des Blitzes aufgeklärt
an den Kreuzwegen das unbeschriebene Pergament
der Schöpfung einatmend
wo Gott wie ein fremder Saft im Blute
seine Herrlichkeit anzeigt.

Walking in the park

Walking in the park—
past the signposts, numbering the constellations
of unrest
where in the hospital wards dying remained lying
having already entered perhaps the hierarchy of higher
   deeds—

now in the open air—
the limbs already beside themselves
to grasp the new age of growth's
lipless language
the rustling—scenting—painting—

The foot instructed in the dream art of hovering
by the exploding power of the dark.

David's dance
in front of the miracle
bearing the budding worlds in the ark of the covenant—

Walking in the park—
the initiated
briefed only by the vocal cords of lightning
breathing in at the crossroad the blank parchment
of creation
where God like a strange sap in the blood
presages his glory.

Sie tanzt

Sie tanzt—
aber mit einem schweren Gewicht—
Warum tanzt sie mit einem schweren Gewicht?
Sie will untröstlich sein—

Ächzend zieht sie ihren Geliebten
am Gelock des Weltmeeres aus der Tiefe
Atem der Unruhe bläst
auf das rettende Gebälk ihrer Arme
Ein leidender Fisch zappelt sprachlos
an ihrer Liebe—

Aber plötzlich
am Genick
Schlaf beugt sie hinüber—

Freigelassene
sind Leben—
sind Tod—

She dances

She dances—
but she dances with a great weight—
Why does she dance with a great weight?
She does not want to be comforted—

Moaning she draws her lover
from the deep by the curls of the world-sea
breath of unrest blows
on the rescuing balks of her arms
A suffering fish struggles speechless
on her love—

But suddenly
at her nape
sleep bends her forward—

The released
are life—
are death—

In ihren Schlafleibern

In ihren Schlafleibern
die Familienqual lagert
böses Schicksal fährt
aus Augen und Händen
eine Gaststätte sind sie
werden gegessen
im Blutpunkt der Nacht.

Wenn Zeit im Zwielicht
ihr Gedächtnis verliert
öffnet sich der Äon in ihren Mündern
bewachsen mit schreiendem Urwald
blitzend mit Zähnen
und es kratzt hinter der Maske
der versandeten Geschlechter Versteck
die auf den Flammenbiss ihrer Gebärerin harren
die mit dem Ende weiterspielt—

The family torment rests

The family torment rests
in their bodies of sleep
evil fate issues
from eyes and hands
they are an inn
are eaten
in the centered blood of night.

When time loses
its memory in the twilight
the aeon opens in their mouths
overgrown with screaming jungle
flashing with teeth
and it scratches behind the mask
hiding place of breeds sunk into oblivion
who wait for the flame bite of the one who bore them
who continues to toy with the end—

Soviel Samenkörner lichtbewurzelt

Soviel Samenkörner lichtbewurzelt
die den Gräbern ihr Geheimnis ausziehen
und es dem Wind überlassen
Prophetenhaar in Feuerzungen einzurätseln
und im weissen Scheiterhaufen des Sterbens
mit allen Blendungen der Wahrheit erscheinen
wenn der Leib nebenan liegt
mit dem Atemrest in der Luft
und rasselnd in der Rückkehr
und eisern verschlossen in der Einsamkeit
mit allen Augen ins Schwarze—

So many seeds rooted with light

So many seeds rooted with light
which draw forth the graves' secret
and leave it to the wind
to riddle prophets' hair into tongues of fire
and appear in the white pyre of dying
with all the dazzlings of truth
when the body lies next door
with the last of breath in the air
and rattling on the road home
and iron-locked in loneliness
with all eyes into darkness—

Da

Da
um die Ecke
und es ist Mitternacht die redet
Bilder gezogen aus schwarzem Gestirn
satanisch Luft musternd
aufgerissene und
am Baum gehenkte Puppen und Larven der Totgeburten
Kaleidoskop der roten Hautwämse
Nachtbehandschuht
Augen nach innen schluckend
Beryll isst das Licht

Im Brunnen mit niemand—
                    verloren—

There

There
round the corner
and it is midnight that speaks
images drawn from black constellations
satanically scrutinizing air
dolls and larvae
of still-births torn open and hung on the tree
kaleidoscope of the red skin jackets
gloved with night
eyes swallowing inward
beryl eats the light

In the well with no one—
                    lost—

Szene aus dem Spiel Nachtwache

Die Augen zu
und dann—
Die Wunde geht auf
und dann—

Man angelt mit Blitzen
O
die Geheimnisse des Blutes
O
für die Fische
Alles im Grab der Luft
Opfer
Henker
Finger
Finger

Das Kind malt im Sarg mit Staub
den Nabel der Welt—
und im Geheg der Zähne hält
der Henker den letzten Fluch—
                        Was nun?

Scene from the Play Nightwatch

Eyes shut
and then—
The wound opens
and then—

One fishes with lightnings
Oh
the mysteries of the blood
Oh
for the fish
All in the grave of air
Victim
Hangman
Finger
Finger

In the coffin the child paints with dust
the navel of the world—
and the hangman holds the last curse
in the stockade of teeth—
                    What now?

Rückwärts

Rückwärts
über alle neunzig Jahre hinweg
gellt die Stimme der Blinden
bis sie eintaucht in Muttermilch
und lichterloh zahnend
über der nächtlichen Bilderstrasse schwebt—
Suchend zwischen unseren Leibern
die Wiege des Staubes
wo die Flügel schlafen—
Ihre Blindenhand
streicht mir die Seele aus dem Leib
vergass nicht meine Stimme
die ihr Antwort gab
gezählt und vermessen
im Klageraum der Litaneien
im Advent des Überganges

Away back

Away back
over all her ninety years
shrills the blind woman's voice
until she dips into mother's milk
and hovers teething and ablaze
above the street of nocturnal images—
Seeking between our bodies
the cradle of dust
where the wings sleep—
Her blind woman's hand
strokes the soul out of my body
did not forget my voice
which answered her
counted and measured out
in the litanies' chamber of lament
in the advent of transition

Eine Negerin lugt—Nachtgeleucht—
aus dem Todkristall—

Überall Zweikampf—
Ein Hund läuft heulend aus der Welt—

Einer ist mit dem Zeichen seiner Angst
durch die Klagemauer gefahren—

Die Erde hat in ihrem Grab aus Feuer
ihr Steinkohlenantlitz gerunzelt—

Hilflos im Schlaf
schmerzt schon Erwachen—

Aber der schwarze Efeu der Lider
scheut noch das Licht—

A Negress peeps—night light

A Negress peeps—night light—
out of death's crystal—

Everywhere single combat—
A dog runs howling from the world—

Someone with his signs of fear
has passed through the wailing wall—

The earth in its grave of fire
has wrinkled its countenance of coal—

Helpless in sleep
even awakening hurts—

But the black ivy of the eyelids
still avoids the light—

Hängend am Strauch der Verzweiflung
und doch auswartend bis die Sage des Blühens
in ihre Wahrsagung tritt—

Zauberkundig
plötzlich der Weisdorn ist ausser sich
vom Tod in das Leben geraten—

Hanging on the bush of despair

Hanging on the bush of despair
and yet enduring until the saga of blossom
fulfills its prophecy—

Magically
the hawthorn is suddenly beside itself
having come from death to life—

Was tut ihr mir

Was tut ihr mir
die mit euch einen Augenwink
da ist im Weltall
Zieht meine Zeit
aus der Lebenden Gesicht
unterjochend die Nacht
und wie Eisen gebogen in flammendes Dasein

Träume aus Wunden

Und der Tag
wo die Sonne eine Blume mir zeichnete
oder einen Stern aus Schnee
Vogelfänger überall
umlauernd Gesang

Aber es ist ja Tod für uns alle bestimmt

Wartet den Atemzug aus
er singt auch für euch

What do you do to me

What do you do to me
who am with you for the flicker of an eyelid
in the universe
Draw my time
from the face of the living
subjugating the night
and like iron bent into flaming existence

Dreams out of wounds

And the day
when the sun sketched me a flower
or a star of snow
bird-catchers everywhere
lying in wait for song

But death is destined for us all

Wait till the breath ends
it will sing for you as well

Grabschrift

Für B.N. und J.M.

Wieder hat einer in der Marter
den weissen Eingang gefunden

Schweigen—Schweigen—Schweigen—

Die innere Sprache erlöst
welch ein Sieg—

Wir pflanzen hier Demut—

Epitaph

For B.N. & J.M.

Someone in torment has again
found the white entrance

Silence—silence—silence—

The inner speech redeems
what a victory—

We plant humility here—

Überall Jerusalem

Am 11. April 1961
In der Trauer

Verborgen ist es im Köcher
und nicht abgeschossen mit dem Pfeil
und die Sonne immer schwarz um das Geheimnis
und gebückt die Sechsunddreissig im Leidenswerk

Aber hier
augenblicklich
ist das Ende—
Alles gespart für das reissende Feuer
Seiner Abwesenheit—

Da
in der Krankheit
gegoren zur Hellsicht
die Prophetin mit dem Stab stösst
auf den Reichtum der Seele

Da ist in der Irre Gold versteckt—

Everywhere Jerusalem

On April 11, 1961
In mourning

It is hidden in the sheath
and not shot down with the arrow
and the sun always black around the secret
and the thirty-six bent in the work of suffering

But here
momentarily
is the end—
Everything saved for the devouring fire
of His absence—

When
in sickness
in a fermented clairvoyance
the prophetess strikes with her staff
the riches of the soul

There in the unknown gold is hidden—

So einsam ist der Mensch

So einsam ist der Mensch
sucht gen Osten
wo die Melancholia im Dämmerungsgesicht erscheint

Rot ist der Osten vom Hähnekrähen

O höre mich—

In der Löwensucht
und im peitschenden Blitz des Äquators
zu vergehn

O höre mich—

Mit den Kindergesichtern der Cherubim zu verwelken
am Abend

O höre mich—

Im blauen Norden der Windrose
wachend zur Nacht
schon eine Knospe Tod auf den Lidern

so weiter zur Quelle—

Man is so lonely

Man is so lonely
searches eastwards
where melancholia appears in the face of dawn

The east is red with cockcrow

Oh hear me—

To die lion-faced
in the equator's whipping lightning

Oh hear me—

To wither with the children's faces of the cherubim
at evening

Oh hear me—

Waking at night in the blue north
of the compass dial
a bud of death already on the eyelids

so on to the source—

Glowing Enigmas: IV

Translated by Michael Hamburger

Verzweiflung
deine Buchstaben wie Streichhölzer
Feuerspeiend
Niemand kommt ans Ende
als durch dein Wortgeweih

Stätte trostlos
Ort des hellen Wahnsinns
bevor er dunkel wird
Nachzügler des Lebens
und Erstling des Sterbens
ohne Hafen
Reissende Sucht
das Geheimnis
des unsichtbaren Messias streifend
mit wildem Heimweh—

Wir stürzten
in das Verliess des Abschieds
rückwärts
schattenschwarz schon
hinausgeschenkt
ins Erloschene—

Despair
your letters like matchsticks
spewing fire
No one reaches his end
but through your branched antler words

Disconsolate site
place of lucid madness
before darkness falls
Straggler of life
and pioneer of dying
with no haven
Sweeping need
Grazing the mystery of
the invisible Messiah
with a wild craving for home—

We rushed
into the dungeon of parting
backwards
shadow-black already
given over
to the extinguished—

Das Meer
sammelt Augenblicke
weiss nichts von Ewigkeit
knotet
das Vier Winde Tuch
in Extase
Tiger und Grille
schlafen im Wiegenlied
der nassen Zeit—

Die Musik
die du hörtest
war eine fremde Musik
Dein Ohr war hinausgerichtet—
Ein Zeichen nahm dich in Anspruch
ass deine Sehweite
kältete dein Blut
stellte Verborgenheit her
zog den Blitz vom Schulterblatt
Du hörtest
Neues

The sea
gathers moments
knows nothing of eternity
knots
the Cloth of Four Winds
in ecstasy
Tiger and cricket
sleep in the lullaby
of wet time—

The music
that you heard
was an alien music
Your ear was turned outward—
A sign claimed your attention
devoured your range of vision
cooled your blood
made you feel hidden
averted the lightning flash from your shoulder blade
You heard
something new

Wieviele Wimpernschläge
als das Grauen kam
kein Lid zum zudrücken
und ein Haufen Zeit versammelt
angemalt auf der Demut der Luft

Dies ist nur mit einem ausgerissenen Auge
aufs Papier zu bringen—

Du hast das Signal gemalt
rot mit deinem Blut
Warnung vor Untergang
an den Grenzen feucht
aber noch ohne Geburt

Wenn das Leiden sich heimatlos niederlässt
stösst es den Überfluss aus
Tränen sind Waisen—Ausgestossene
im Sprung folgen wir nach
das ist die Flucht ins Jenseits
der wurzellosen Zeitpalme—

How many blinkings of eyelashes
when horror came
no eyelid to be lowered
and a heap of time put together
painted over the air's humility

This can be put on paper only
with one eye ripped out—

You painted the signal
red with your blood
warning of destruction
moist on the borders
but still without birth

When suffering settles homeless
it expels superfluity
Tears are orphans—expelled
in one bound we follow
that is flight into the Beyond
of the rootless palm tree of time—

Einmal
als Abend im Rot den Tag vergass
gründete ich auf dem Stein der Schwermut
die Zukunft

Vorgeburtliches Wiedersehen—
eine Melodie aus Meer gemacht
lief ihre Bahn—

Vielleicht ein Fisch am Äquator
an der Angel eine Menschenschuld bezahlte
und dann mein Du
das man gefangen hielt
und das zu retten ich erkoren war
und das in Rätseln weiter ich verlor
bis hartes Schweigen sich auf Schweigen senkte
und eine Liebe ihren Sarg bekam—

So kurz ausgeliefert ist der Mensch
wer kann da über Liebe sprechen
das Meer hat längere Worte
auch die kristallgefächerte Erde
mit weissagendem Wuchs
Dieses leidende Papier
schon krank vom Staub-zum Staube-Lied
das gesegnete Wort entführend
vielleicht zurück zu seinem magnetischen Punkt
der Gottdurchlässig ist—

Once
when in the redness evening forgot the day
I founded
the future upon the stone of sadness

Prenatal reunion—
a time made of ocean
ran its course—

Perhaps near the equator a fish
on the line paid off a human debt
and then my Thou
who was kept a prisoner
and whom to release I was chosen
and whom in enigmas I lost once more
until hard silence descended on silence
and a love was granted its coffin—

So briefly delivered up is humankind
who then can speak of love
the ocean has longer words
and so has the crystal-fanned Earth
with prophetic growth
This suffering paper
sick already with the Song of Dust to Dust
carrying off the blessed word
perhaps back to its magnetic point
which is permeable by God—

Man darf sich nicht erlauben
so zu leiden
sagte der Seher von Lublin
und jedes Wort
von Mitternacht durchkreuzt
schlaflos gewendet
hörtest du es anderswo
vielleicht
wo ein Mass für Masslosigkeit erfunden war
Liebe vom Erdenstoff befreit
die Meteorensprache
verboten einem Stern
und selber warst du ausser dir
du Seher von Lublin—

One must not permit oneself
to suffer *so*
said the seer of Lublin
and every word
crisscrossed with midnight
sleeplessly turned over
you heard elsewhere
perhaps
where a measure was found for immoderation
Love freed from earthly matter
the language of meteors
forbidden to a star
and you yourself were beside yourself
you seer of Lublin—

Diese Jahrtausende
geblasen vom Atem
immer um ein zorniges Hauptwort kreisend
aus dem Bienenkorb der Sonne
stechende Sekunden
kriegerische Angreifer
geheime Folterer

Niemals eine Atempause wie in Ur
da ein Kindervolk an den weissen Bändern zog
mit dem Mond Schlafball zu spielen—

Auf der Strasse mit Windeseile
läuft die Frau
Medizin zu holen für das kranke Kind

Vokale und Konsonanten
schreien in allen Sprachen:
H i l f e !

These millennia
blown by the breath
always in orbit around an angry noun
out of the sun's beehive
stinging seconds
warlike aggressors
secret torturers

Never a breathing space as in Ur
when a people of children tugged at the white ribbons
to play sleep-ball with the moon—

In the street with wind's haste
the woman runs
to fetch medicine for the sick child

Vowels and consonants
cry out in every language:
H e l p !

Ich bin meinem Heimatrecht auf der Spur
dieser Geographie nächtlicher Länder
wo die zur Liebe geöffneten Arme
gekreuzigt an den Breitengraden hängen
bodenlos in Erwartung—

Es ist ein Schwarz wie
Chaos vor dem Wort
Leonardo suchte dieses Schwarz
hinter dem Schwarz
Hiob war eingewickelt
in den Geburtenleib der Sterne
Jemand schüttelt die Schwärze
bis der Apfel Erde fällt
gereift ans Ende
Ein Seufzer
ist das die Seele—?

I'm on the track of my rights of domicile
this geography of nocturnal countries
where the arms opened for love
hang crucified on the degrees of latitude
groundless in expectation—

It is a black like
chaos before the word
Leonardo looked for that black
behind black
Job was swaddled
in the life-bearing body of the stars
Someone shakes the blackness
till the apple Earth drops
ripened to its end
A sigh
is that the soul—?

Immer auf der schiefen Ebene
wo alles entfällt-rollt
in den Ab-grund
das fahrende-stehende Wort
vom Schweigen zu Tode getroffen
und wieder aufbricht
das Samenkorn der Nacht
im Schauder der neuen Sprache
hineingeflüstert
in die Wurzelblätter des Planeten
vor der Morgenröte—

Always on the tilted plane
where everything falls away—rolls
into the abyss
the moving-standing word
mortally struck by silence
and the seed grain of night
bursts open again
amid the new language's tremor
whispered into
the root leaves of the planet
before sunrise—

Der hervorstürzende
Fackelzug der Ahnen
in den Ysophgärten schimmerten ihre Köpfe
in den Verstecken des Blutes landsflüchtig den Gott
Auf den Küsten der Mitternacht
auf den verbannten Inseln
getauft mit den Wetterfahnen des Blitzes
Agonie in brennenden Tempeln
eure Heimat in meine Adern verlegt—

Reich bin ich wie das Meer
aus Vergangenheit und Zukunft
und ganz aus Sterbestoff
singe ich euer Lied—

The outrushing
torchlight procession of ancestors
in the hyssop gardens their heads glittered
in the blood's hiding places fleeing the country the God
On the shores of midnight
on the banished islands
baptized with the weather vanes of lightning
Agony in burning temples
Your home removed into my arteries—

Rich I am as the ocean
of past and future
and wholly of mortal stuff
I sing your song—